OVERSEAS PROPERTY GUIDE

The Daily Telegraph

OVERSEAS PROPERTY GUIDE

DAVID HOPPIT

Published by Telegraph Publications
Peterborough Court, At South Quay, 181 Marsh Wall, London E14 9SR

First published February 1986
Second edition 1988
© The Daily Telegraph/William Curtis Ltd 1988

British Library Cataloguing in Publication Data
Hoppit, David
Overseas property guide
1. Overseas residence. For Britons
I. Title
910'2'02

ISBN 0-86367-205-1

Typeset by Addenda (Sales & Marketing) Limited, Reading, Berks
Printed and bound by Butler & Tanner, Frome

CONTENTS

PART III

Introduction

Despite all the gloomy forecasts, the threat of a nuclear winter, trade deficits, AIDS, and all the other prophecies of doom and gloom which are constantly arrayed before us, we live in a relatively affluent society. There is high unemployment and the state of our heritage of housing is causing genuine concern, but social historians will probably remember the twentieth century for what is left of the National Health Service and the phenomenal growth in home ownership, with the wealth this has created for individual citizens. Huge sums are being inherited as a result of our property-owning democracy.

Half a century ago a holiday home was the prerogative of the rich, many of whom undertook arduous journeys to distant sporting estates in Scotland for a little salmon fishing (there were more fish then) or to bag a few brace of grouse on the 'Glorious Twelfth', but what a palaver it all was. Nancy Astor even had her favourite cow transported to Jura during family holidays so that she could get the daily 'pinta' of her choice.

Communications, plus a change in the social order, have made the world smaller and brought holidays and the ownership of holiday homes within reach of many more ordinary people. We have more leisure time too, and as package holidays are no longer the amazing bargains they once were, the ownership of a holiday home becomes all the more attractive. Even those who cannot afford a second home now have the opportunity for holiday investment that did not exist a decade ago. Time-sharing and holiday property bonds for instance, with their built-in capacity for exchange, are in some ways preferable to outright ownership.

It has been estimated that one in every 150 English families owns a second home somewhere in Great Britain. This has inevitably led to some anti-social trends, not least of which has been the gradual death of the community spirit in those villages which are the weekend 'honeypots' of city workers. In one Cotswold village all but four of the cottages are normally empty from Monday to Friday.

In addition to this domestic phenomenon there are the many thousands of families who for one reason or another seek a foothold abroad; most wanting a more dependable sunshine record. Added to this is the growing army of timesharers, 'time-lords' as I once called them, who own periods of time at luxury resorts around the world and who use that ownership as a stepping-stone to

THE BEST PROPERTY ADVICE ABROAD

IS HERE AT HOME

If you're buying property abroad, the first thing you need is advice from the experts — Prudential International Property. We have offices and associates in Spain, Mallorca, the Canaries, Portugal, France, Italy, Switzerland, Turkey and Cyprus. So we know the scene over there.

But we're also thick on the ground over here, with International Sales Centres offering more property and expertise than anyone in the UK. Call us at:

PRUDENTIAL
International Property

9 Heath Street, Hampstead NW3 6TP. Tel: 01-435 3864

Other offices also at: Altrincham Tel: 061-941 4491
Reading Tel: 0734 585181 Nottingham Tel: 0602 484226

explore new areas. The number of British families owning a slice of the time-share cake reached 120,000 in 1987, by which time there were 50 domestic developments to choose from. Worldwide well over a million families now enjoy time-sharing holidays at more than 2000 different resorts, most of them opting for the ability to exchange their holidays with fellow owners.

Modern-day thrift is not cash in a shoe-box under the bed - inflation has made a nonsense of that sort of saving! We should put our pennies and pounds into bricks and mortar, or into a pension fund that will buy us bricks and mortar in the years to come. Home-buyers' rush to purchase property abroad in recent years, especially since exchange controls were lifted, has not always been prudent, and some have regretted what they have done. It surprises me how few tears have been shed, and this is to some extent due to a new and more responsible attitude among developers and estate agents.

This book is not a substitute for sound professional advice, which is as essential today as it ever was; it seeks to identify common problems and be an aid to the reader when buying property. There are still rogues in the world whose smile turns to a leer once the contract is signed. We are offering a pair of spectacles to assist your vision in the overseas property market. Good hunting, and may your glass be never empty!

PART I

Chapter One: Motives and Decisions

The cheapest house in Great Britain in the mid-1980s was a little mid-terrace cottage in Wales, complete with a new roof, two bedrooms and an indoor privy. The price was just £700 (no I haven't left a nought off). Within hours of publication of the story in my Wednesday property column more than a thousand people had contacted the agent wanting to buy it. For a few days the Victorian miner's cottage was the most famous house in the land, so popular in fact that the estate agent was forced to close his office until normality returned to the valleys.

This may seem at first glance a somewhat off-beat way to begin a book about holiday and retirement home opportunities, but the story demonstrates just how strong the demand is for second homes; almost all of those callers saw the Welsh cottage as the solution to their future holiday problems. The paradox is that at a time when many young people are struggling to get a foot on the first rung of the property ladder, more and more of us are on the look-out for an affordable second home.

There is nothing new about dreaming of a second home, a sanctuary away from the stress of modern living. Roman aristocrats were certainly doing it 2000 years ago, and for all we know Stone Age chiefs had a favourite cave by the sea for summer use. The difference today is that even plebeians aspire to amass enough surplus capital to purchase at least a share in a holiday home, be it a villa in Marbella, a croft in Scotland, or just a week or two in a time-share development.

Not that everyone has the same motives for wanting to invest in another property. The majority see a second home as an appreciating asset offering inflation-proof holiday accommodation. If the worst comes to the worst it can always be sold, and probably at a handsome profit. Package holidays, on the other hand, are no longer the bargains they were, and as children get older the cost becomes greater.

Others buy a second home in the sun as a short-term solution for holidays but with a view to eventual retirement there. The third category of buyer is the investor, more interested in capital growth than he is in ambience. The last

11

group can include rogues who see the purchase of bricks and mortar overseas as a convenient and near-foolproof way of laundering their ill-gotten gains. This is one of the less attractive sides of the story, the risk that you may well be living next-door to a bank robber. Fortunately, Spain, which is one of the main choices for self-imposed exile, has negotiated a restoration of the former extradition agreement with Great Britain and so the rogues should no longer be able to cock a snook at the law from the comfort of a deckchair beside the pool.

This book is really intended for the first two categories, in particular the buyers who are considering a second home in the sun, one that will eventually become their full-time home. Buying overseas is one thing but severing all ties with the mother-country and moving lock, stock and barrel is quite another and requires very careful planning indeed. In Part I we point out a few of the more obvious pros and cons of buying overseas. It is not that we think all foreigners are rogues, quite the reverse in fact, but simply that their rules and customs are often very different from our own.

Part II deals with some countries most often considered for suitable investments. Naturally it is not practical to give a detailed analysis of every possible destination and so we have concerned ourselves with the main areas. If you want to buy an igloo in Greenland, or a mud hut in Borneo, this is unfortunately not the book for you. It also has to be said that whilst the countries included are currently politically stable, national laws and politics can change overnight.

One of the difficulties in a guide of this kind is that by the time it is published some of the facts may already be out of date. Inflation is not just a British phenomenon; therefore prices of property given in the country information section are as up to date as inflation allows. Use these prices therefore as a guide.

Whilst every country has its own rules, there are certain basic guidelines which apply wherever and whenever you buy property. Some may sound obvious, even presumptuous, but I never cease to be surprised by the foolish things otherwise intelligent people do when they are out of their own natural environment. A combination of excess sunshine and Rioja has produced many regrets. Those famous inspection trips are all very well in their own way, but always insist upon a 'cooling off' period before you commit your signature to any contract or before you part with the family fortune.

Professional advice

This brings me to inspection trips. These trips are sometimes subsidised and often agents and developers will offer the carrot of a complete refund on them in the event of a purchase. The agents' success rate on these jolly trips is, in most regions, very high; but on the other side of the coin there are some people who simply have a weekend in the sun with no intention of ever buying. In most cases, unless the potential buyer is very thick-skinned, there is a moral commitment to look only at what the host agent is showing. Inspection trips serve as a useful back-up, but do look carefully at what all the agents have to offer before deciding which, if any, is right for you.

How do you find reputable agents? Not all the reputable agents belong to the umbrella organisations, but all those that do belong should be reputable. It follows that I recommend those that are affiliated to such associations as the Association of British Overseas Property Agents (ABOPA) and the Federation of Overseas Property Developers, Agents and Consultants (FOPDAC). The addresses of the associations are noted in Part III. I must stress that this does not mean that an agent who chooses to dissociate himself from such organisations is disreputable, only that it is one extra safeguard potential buyers might wish to take.

FOPDAC has three types of membership. Full members are well established firms of good repute; provisional members are firms that are on trial; while associate members include lawyers, financial experts and removal specialists. The Federation started 12 years ago, and while no British based organisation can be held responsible for the iniquities of overseas developers, the members, like those in ABOPA, can advise on how best to avoid pitfalls. It is interesting to note that very few of the agents operating 15 years ago are still in business, but quite a few of those operating 10 years ago have survived.

My advice on the subject of lawyers is simple - never attempt to buy property without using one. Just as in England it is possible to do your own thing, so it is in deepest Spain, but the saving is not worth the aggravation. Even so, many people who would not sign anything in England without first consulting their lawyer have signed away their life-savings when abroad. The victims include accountants and even lawyers.

However I do think that the legal person you appoint should have a specialist knowledge of the area, or at least the country in which you plan to invest. Therefore go to a specialist firm or, better still a reputable lawyer or a Notary who is based in the region in which you have chosen to buy property and who speaks English.

One of the most useful things you can do is talk to as many people as possible who have bought property in either the area, or the development, in which you are interested. Ask questions and listen to their opinions. They can often mention a valid point which you have not even thought of. Buying a house can be fun but it can also be a traumatic experience so do not make any spur of the moment decisions.

The 'Ten Commandments' of property purchase

To assist would-be purchasers of property, I have drawn up a list of priorities which I have found over the years to represent good, practical advice. Some are quite obvious whereas others fall into the category of 'Gosh, I didn't think of that'.

Commandment number one: do not rush in until you are absolutely certain that you have found your own private holiday Utopia. A brief holiday in a resort is not, in my view, sufficient test of suitability. Even a series of holidays can leave one with a misleading impression of an area's true characteristics. Bliss for the gregarious sun-lover could be misery in the winter when both sun and people are gone. Alternatively, someone enjoying the peace and quiet of April might be in for a shock when the holiday season begins and flocks of tourists descend. Wise people buy a 'stepping-stone' house, a small property perhaps even a mobile home (now more commonly referred to as 'park homes'), before committing the entire family fortune.

Number two of our Ten Commandments concerns the professionals - the agent, whose livelihood depends upon you and others like you deciding to buy, and the solicitor, who in his own way also depends for his income upon people like you purchasing property. Agents do not enjoy the most flattering of images, largely because of unscrupulous operators of yesteryear, particularly during the period when exchange controls made the purchase of overseas property so impractical. Many people lost their lifesavings after handing over a suitcase stuffed with cash to a total stranger in a hotel foyer in London, believing it would be used to buy that long-awaited villa. When the title deeds did not materialise nothing could be done for the victim as he had been trying to circumnavigate the law. Those days are past, but we may not always have a Conservative Government in office which is committed to the present policy. There are those in Westminster who would like to see exchange controls introduced once more, and this would frustrate the aspirations of many people.

Exchange controls begat shady deals, and shady deals begat shady agents. These days there is really no temptation to break the rules - the savings would be small and the possible consequences, if a resale became necessary, might prove embarrassing - and so most agents must play by the rules to survive. They are, nevertheless, dependent upon regular sales for their survival, so do not be gullible; even if the salesman did have an honest face and a nice smile, he could still be trying to sell you something which is not quite right for you. If the lunch he bought you was excellent, remember that four people can eat like kings in Portugal for the price of one mediocre meal in London. The rule here is, do not be tempted until you are absolutely sure that it is the place you want, at the price you can afford.

Commandment number three: study the rules and customs of your chosen country most carefully, for they can differ greatly from the ones you know and understand. Especially important are arrangements for pensions, medical care and wills, but above all, it is essential for peace of mind to be certain that you can get your money out of the country if, after a year or two, it transpires that you have made a horrible mistake and the green fields of Suffolk were better after all. Wills, pensions and medical insurances are covered in Chapter 3. Each country has its own rules on repatriation of money, and most have some form of capital gains tax on profits from sales that are deemed unacceptable. Again we will attempt to explain these rules and regulations country by country. If you intend to work it may be necessary to apply for a work permit, and these are not always forthcoming. In some countries you will need a permanent resident visa if you are going to live there for more than six months.

Which brings me to Commandment number four; with the possible exception of Italy, where curious manipulations of the rules have become normal practice it seems, always register the correct price that you are paying for your villa or apartment. There is really very little to be gained by deceiving the notary and putting a lower figure on the title deeds. If you do, and in due course you decide to sell up and return to Great Britain, the profit you make from the sale will appear all the larger and the capital gains tax will, *ipso facto*, be larger too. It is vital to the house purchaser that money is transferred correctly and through the normal traditional banking channels. If this is not observed then repatriation of that money, in the event of a sale, could be prejudiced.

Number five of our Ten Commandments concerns title to your new home. Again, each country has its own arrangements for property registration and this is really why professional legal advice *must* be sought. It is essential that you ascertain who is the rightful owner of the property and that no other party, be it a bank, builder or distant nephew of the vendor, has any claim. It is too late after the contracts have been signed and money exchanged. If a villa is standing in its own ground, then there should be no delay, in most countries, to getting proper title. However, there might be a delay in the case of a flat with the remaining block still under construction. In this case you must insist your solicitor obtain some form of certificate of ownership. Check also when buying older property, that there are no outstanding bills attached to it - the debts of the previous incumbent may be visited upon the next.

Commandment six. Most people who buy a brand new apartment or villa either choose it from a plan or, at best, see it when the development is only half finished. Supposing the builder goes bankrupt after you have paid him some, or worst still, all of your money? Spanish law now requires a developer to offer buyers a guarantee of completion, usually backed by a bank or insurance company. Unfortunately not all developers abide by this particular law. I would be inclined to trust a developer who had the sound backing of a bank, and even then I would part with money only at agreed stages, payment linked not to dates but to actual progress in building . . . so much at each footing level, so much when the roof is on, and so on until the key is handed over. Then ensure that he will put right any niggling problems associated with its construction.

Number seven is: beware of glossy brochures and smiling developers telling of the plans for further phases of development - the marina he will build, the squash courts, tennis courts, and swimming pools, not to mention the disco and restaurant. Steer yourselves towards a developer who puts his money, as the agents say, 'up front'; in other words he completes the infrastructure and many of the facilities early on in the building operations.

Commandment number eight concerns integration. At least have a crack at learning the local language, as the local people will be much more ready to embrace you into their community if you attempt to communicate, and that means in their own language rather than shouting in English. It pays not to alienate your new neighbours. They may own the access to your villa, or control the local water supply! The time will almost certainly come when you will need the help of the local community, and you may also need a gardener, cook and maid. If you have not learnt the language, and they cannot speak English, then you will soon find out how difficult communication is when using sign language!

Number nine of our Ten Commandments concerns logistics. Unless you plan to visit your home only once a year it is vital that you choose an easily accessible place. If you have a family then it is also important to concern yourself with the cost of air tickets. When an air ticket has been quadrupled the point sinks home. A useful book to read is the Telegraph Publications' *A Consumer's Guide to Air Fares*. Do carefully consider cost and ease of access. A Londoner can be in the Canary Islands in less time than it takes him to drive to Scotland but it could cost him more. These points could greatly affect the letting potential of your second home. For me, the joy of a second home would be the ability it would afford me to escape at a moment's notice. To be able to drop everything, get into the car or buy a ticket, and be in my own home within two or three hours - ah, well!

Lastly, and most important, do not overstretch the family funds and whatever happens keep within the law of the country. Prisons and punishments in other countries are not always as civilised as ours, so I am told!

Living with one's spouse in another country can put enormous strain on a hitherto tranquil relationship. It is perhaps an unsavoury subject to discuss here and to end a chapter on, but the endless round of cocktails, coupled with cheap liquor and boredom, has caused many a divorce.

These commandments are ones which I have found, and observed, to be those which need due attention. However, there may be others which you consider important in the successful purchase of your second home. Add them to these and you will go a long way towards ensuring that you are buying a home in which you can be very happy and not one which could cause a financial burden or become a nightmare.

Chapter Two: Time-share, Property Bonds and the Like

There are several alternatives to outright ownership of a property, not least of which is time-sharing, or multi-ownership as it is sometimes called. For very much less than it costs to buy that cottage, flat or villa, someone with only a limited capital outlay can buy a week or two at a development which offers luxury verging on opulence, usually with built-in leisure and sports facilities of the highest standard.

During the past year or two the very word 'time-sharing' has become synonymous with 'rip-off'; this is a shame because of course the vast majority of companies are anxious to foster an image of responsibility. It takes only a couple of rogues to tarnish the image of the rest. Practically all the adverse publicity has been the result of aggressive sales tactics by OPCs (off-property contacts). People have been pestered from the moment they landed at an airport to begin their holiday, and many have signed contracts they later regretted. One of the problems has been the fragmentation of the industry; until recently no fewer than three separate organisations claimed to represent the consumer, but none had any real powers. Now at last they have got together and formed the Timeshare Developers Association; eventually, one hopes, it will be impossible for a developer to operate without TDA membership, but for the time being it is at least a step in the right direction. The codes of conduct drawn up by the new organisation include a cooling off period, during which people may withdraw from any contract they have signed, and a ban on hard pressure selling by OPCs in such places as bars, beaches or poolsides.

This concept of time-sharing took a long time to become established in Great Britain, largely because of our natural caution and suspicion of anything that is new, or innovative, or which seems too good to be true. A bias still exists, even among many estate agents and others concerned with property. When people say, 'it doesn't appeal to me', I usually discover, after only a short conversation, that they have no understanding of the subject.

Time-sharing is the purchase of the right to use a property at a chosen time of the year, or in some cases, it is the purchase of an actual share in the freehold of the property. That time, which is usually priced according to the season, can

be exchanged at resorts in many other parts of the world, and it can also be bequeathed, let, or sold on.

The man who introduced time-sharing to our shores was Mr Frank Chapman whose first venture, overlooking the beautiful Loch Rannoch in Scotland, is now practically sold out. That bold undertaking 11 years ago set high standards, both in terms of location and finish, towards which others had to strive if they were to succeed.

Our time-share industry has benefited from its relatively slow start by learning from mistakes made by other 'time-lords' around the world. While one or two developments have failed over the years, I know of no-one who has lost any money or been greatly inconvenienced. This is a commendable record when one considers the tears that were shed in the early days of package tours.

Frank Chapman's leisure empire continued to grow, and it has now been absorbed into the great Barratt house-building machine. Indeed, Barratt Multi-Ownership is one of the more successful arms of the company. Other resorts have been acquired or taken over. These new resorts are in Scotland, Wales and England, but also in the south of Spain.

After a slow start, the time-share industry suddenly shot up in the popularity stakes, with new developments appearing almost every week. Now we seem to have reached a plateau with about 40 really good developments in Great Britain. This is a relatively small number when compared with a worldwide total approaching 1500, but it puts owners in a strong position when they want to exchange their weeks. There are more people wanting to come to Europe from America than there are units for them. For this reason one of the exchange clubs is offering British owners two weeks in America for every one week that they own in Great Britain - all you have to find, of course, is the fares.

It has always been my philosophy that one should buy periods of time-sharing at developments in one's own country. This is not because of any blazing patriotism on my part, but because it is so much easier to keep an eye on the investment. If problems do arise they can be more easily solved, the language is familiar and there are no worries about currency fluctuation. Also, if fares rise sharply, or strikes disrupt travel, access to the holiday home here in the UK is so much easier. One misconception that I have already mentioned is the mistaken belief that an owner is committed to a holiday at the same resort year in, year out.

The two main exchange networks, Interval International (II) based in Gilmoora House, 57/61 Mortimer Street, London WIN 7TD and Resort Condominiums International of Parnell House, 19/28 Wilton Road, London SW1V 1LW claim success rates of well above 90 per cent in satisfying members' requests. (RCI last year reported a figure of 98.5 per cent.) Most developments offer buyers free membership for between one and five years of the network to which they are affiliated. Thereafter families pay an annual membership of £38

(with discounts for those paying three or five years in advance) for RCI, or £42 for II with reductions for multiple year membership, plus a fee for the exchange. RCI charges £40 for every week swapped (or £22 if the week is within the same resort); while II has an exchange fee of £42, but if two or more weeks run consecutively and the same resort is acceptable, then members pay just £63.

Worldwide there are now perhaps as many as a million families with a slice of the time-share cake, and many of them make use of the exchange clubs. So far as Great Britain is concerned the pattern seems to be that families choose their resort and then visit it for the first few holidays, and eventually, after about four years, become more adventurous and swap for somewhere else. This is perhaps sensible for families with young children for there is a lot to be said for returning to familiar pastures. For the unencumbered, however, time-share offers the opportunity to buy time at a luxurious development in the low season, perhaps for not much more than £1000 a week, and then swap to a low season holding in somewhere like Switzerland, or the Seychelles, which are quite nice all the year round. In some cases Interval International can arrange to swap low season for high season, but generally speaking this is rarely possible. Since there are now so many resorts around the world from which to choose, a time-sharer can truly claim the world is his oyster - his money has bought a stepping-stone to the sort of holiday that would be beyond most people's pocket.

The year of 1985 was something of a milestone in the British time-share industry. It saw the completion of the first decade of trading during which remarkably few problems have arisen. In 1985 the number of British owners rose to 50,000 and sales to British investors during the year topped £76 million, half the total spent during the first ten years. Now, three years later the number of British families owning weeks is at least 120,000 and annual purchases in 1987 alone topped £250 million.

Throughout this chapter I refer to the 'investor' meaning the person who buys time at a development. It cannot be stressed too strongly that the investment factor is not necessarily one of capital growth. People who bought weeks at some of the early developments have indeed seen the value of their weeks soar, but this situation may not continue. Indeed, there is always the possibility that values could fall though this is unlikely to happen at the better-established developments.

Time-sharing is not an investment for capital growth; rather, as the developers' panegyric reassures us, it offers 'inflation-proof holidays for life'. It is a long-term holiday investment, and anyone who thinks they may need their money back quickly should look for alternative places to put it. We are, however, talking about a relatively small amount of money; less perhaps than one might spend on a second car which will almost certainly fall dramatically in value, leaving you with nothing but bills and a pile of rust.

Time-sharers do have some bills, of course. They pay an annual charge for every week they own, currently averaging about £75, depending upon the standard of luxury and range of facilities. Check that owners have control over the management, so that if the managing company becomes spendthrift, or incompetent, it can be fired.

They also have to consider logistics. This is another reason for my own preference for buying British. However, it seems that I am in a minority; according to official statistics nearly seven out of ten Britons buying time-share weeks are content to buy at an overseas resort. There are plenty to choose from, it is true, and the general standards are remarkably high. Standards have to be high for the exchange clubs to allow membership. My fear is that if those standards do start to fall, the clubs may be forced to disaffiliate some developments, thus removing the ability of owners within these developments to exchange their allocation. Perhaps I am being hypercautious, but I feel that such an unlikely occurrence would be even less likely if owners buy in their own country and have closer control over the destiny of their development.

There are almost as many different styles of time-sharing as there are developments, each having its own particular character. One especially heartening aspect of the growth of the leisure industry is the new role that our heritage of great houses can play. Many are now host to a multitude of owners who live like lords for the duration of their time there.

First of the stately homes to be turned over to time-sharing was Broome Park, near Canterbury. A Grade I listed building, it dates from 1635 and is said to be one of the finest Charles I houses; it was once the home of Lord Kitchener. The grounds cover about 113 hectares (280 acres): ample room for a golf course and many other facilities. Most of the apartments are now fully sold, but there are still available 26 Regency-style villas which sleep at least six people. Elsewhere in Britain prices range between £1200 and £16,500, the latter being at The Marina in Salcombe. Among the other notable houses to be transformed in this way is Brantridge Park, a Grade II listed building near Haywards Heath in West Sussex. This was once the home of Princess Alice of Athlone. Up in Yorkshire there is Sutton Hall near Thirsk, while not far from Stratford-upon-Avon there is Walton Hall, a Grade II Victorian mansion designed by Sir Gilbert Scott in grand Gothic-revival style.

Not only stately homes have proved suitable for time-share development. Humble cottages in Tresco on the Isles of Scilly, or at a former gunpowder factory in the wild Loch Melfort area of Scotland, are proving extremely popular, as is a range of lichen-covered former farm buildings called Court Barton near Salcombe in Devon.

The Court Barton development has proved popular partly because of its location and high standards, but also because of this element of ownership which some others cannot always give. The laws relating to time-share vary from country to country; in Scotland, for instance, weeks are sold in perpetuity, whereas in England and Wales a long lease is all that is permitted.

One of the most exciting stately home conversions is at Walton Hall, a few miles from Stratford-upon-Avon, where the purchase of one or more weeks automatically gives an all the year round membership to an exclusive country club. Additionally, the weeks are sold on a share system, like those at Court Barton, so that at the end of the 25-year period a democratic decision is taken and either the entire estate is sold off and the proceeds shared or the status quo is continued. Apartments exhibit the ultimate in luxury, and facilities include horse riding, squash, tennis, and more gentle pursuits like croquet and whirl-pool bathing.

The Grade II mansion, designed by Sir Gilbert Scott in grand Gothic-revival style, stands in 26 hectares (65 acres) of parkland, with the village chapel nearby. So far, many of the investors have been local people wanting the facilities that the country club offers while probably intending to use their weeks to exchange for holidays at other resorts around the world. There are health and beauty facilities, a notable wine cellar, and a praiseworthy chef. In addition there are no fewer than 17 sports catered for including trout fishing in the huge lake. The price of all this excellence is between £2750 and about £9000 for each week bought, depending upon the size of the unit and the time of year reserved. The maintenance charge, currently runs at between £110 and £130 for each week owned.

Some hotels have also seen the wisdom of converting a few of their suites into time-shared accommodation, notably the old Osborne, that south coast landmark in Torquay, and the fine Carlton Hotel in Bournemouth. If skiing and mountain air are more to your liking there is a Scandinavian Village and Barratt's Dalfaber developments in Aviemore, Scotland, not itself a pretty village but a good jumping off point for exploring.

Perhaps the most successful development of all has been that at Langdale in the Lake District, another development that is on the site of a former gunpowder works (last used in 1928). Like that at Melfort, whose works closed after a disastrous explosion last century, some of the old buildings have been preserved. The streams which once turned the huge mill-stones now form an essential part of the landscaping at Langdale, even flowing past the gourmets in the best restaurant. Since it opened in 1982, some 2500 weeks have been sold in the 56 lodges built so far. A further 22 lodges have still to be completed, the best, in my view, beside the roaring beck that forms a natural boundary to the development. Facilities, including a huge swimming pool, squash courts, beauty salons and so on, are of the highest standard. Lodges vary in size, but weeks start at £1500 plus VAT for the smallest and in low season, rising to £7750 per week plus VAT for the largest in high season. Langdale was the first real time-share development in the Lake District, but now there are others. A worthy rival is being built at the old Dolly Blue factory in the village of Beckbarrow, on the banks of the River Leven.

One of the latest and most promising developments in Scotland, where tourism is so important to the economy, is Craigendarroch in the beautiful and under-exploited Deeside. It is almost next door to Balmoral, and just above the swiftly flowing river so loved by the royal family. Buyers have the satisfaction of knowing that all the facilities have been provided 'up front', and they do not have to wait a few years for the swimming pool, or curling rink. A total of 83 lodges will be built on the 28-acre wooded site with weeks costing between £1600 and £8500 per week. This is a lovely area for a holiday, with outdoor sports including fishing and gliding, plenty of facilities at the site itself, with the Glenfiddich Distillery not far away - such nice neighbours too!

There are several alternatives to time-sharing if outright ownership is beyond your financial grasp. Indeed the forerunner of time-sharing was a Swiss-based company known as Hapimag, though this rather frivolous-sounding name is actually an acronym for Hotel Apartment und Immobilienanlage Aktiengesellschaft. The company, formed by a German, Alexander Nette, in 1963, now has a paid-up capital of more than £9 million. Hapimag has a total membership of above 50,000 but only recently ventured into Great Britain, where it now has more than 2500 members. They have a collective interest in nearly 40 resorts in 11 European countries, including Finland and Greece, where it is not always possible to buy property. The company's portfolio of properties was recently extended to include Dunrobin Castle near Golspie in Sutherland, but it will be at least another year before the castle and the period-style village of 150 new cottages will be available for holidays. The Countess of Sutherland will retain one-third of the castle as the clan centre.

Hapimag's members buy shares in the company, the more they have the greater the duration and flexibility of their holidays. The club works on a points system, one share currently costing £2000 giving 12 points. When the club started in 1963 a share cost only £100, so the annual growth in value of shares has been in the order of 13 per cent. Shares can be bequeathed or sold, but there is a small charge to cover administration in the event of a sale.

Naturally a family can own more than one share. A family with just 12 points might expect two or even three weeks at a resort in low season, but a week at high season on the French Riviera would use up 24 points. Points can be saved up, and members can even borrow them - a sort of points-overdraft. Thus a family with four shares (48 points) would be assured of a two week holiday at high season for evermore, or at least 12 weeks at low season. For me the big advantage of this club is the entré it gives to some of the more unusual destinations, such as the Black Forest, and Finland where foreigners cannot easily buy property. Altogether the club owns about 2000 villas, apartments and chalets in Europe.

There are further alternatives to outright ownership. There is, for example, the Holiday Property Bond, being sold through the Villa Owners' Club based in Newmarket, Suffolk. To date some 1600 people have invested about £6 million in the scheme, and a total of 50 properties in a dozen different European locations have been bought. These include the Canary Islands, Cyprus, Portugal, Spain, France and, of course, Great Britain. The fund is growing rapidly with about £750,000 being invested every month. New destinations include Florida, Tuscany and Greece. Unfortunately HPB has complicated the excellent scheme by introducing two categories of bond: gold and silver, an unnecessary and confusing innovation. Nevertheless HPB is destined to become one of the best holiday investments so far devised.

The minimum investment is £1000, with each pound buying one point. The investor can save up his points for two years. While a week's holiday can be had for just 1000 points in low season, most buyers have opted for a larger investment of around £5000. A holiday for two weeks in high season at Rocha-Brava, in Portugal, would use up 4320 points. This unit has been specially adapted for use by both able-bodied and disabled members as have several others in similar resorts. There are no management charges, and here, as with Hapimag, the members' investments can actually rise in value year by year.

These then are just a few of the opportunities for holiday investment which Mr and Mrs Average can certainly aspire to. I believe that future holiday patterns will involve schemes such as these where a once-only capital investment secures a permanent holiday arrangement. The traditional package holiday, with all its unpredictable headaches, could be on the way out.

Chapter Three: All the Necessary Essentials

The wealthy Midlands businessman was quite precise about the dimensions of the villa he wanted built in the south of Spain. He instructed his architect to allow for an 18 foot kitchen and a 25 foot lounge, while outside there was to be a barbecue and a 30 foot swimming pool.

During construction he was surprised by the regular demands for 'more pesetas - more pesetas'. Eventually the great day arrived for him to take his wife for her first glimpse of their new home in the sun. And there it was, with an 18 metre kitchen, a 25 metre lounge and a 30 metre swimming pool!

Absurd but true - it demonstrates rather well the sort of ridiculous misunderstanding that can occur when dealing with far-away people in far-away places. Eventually, I understand, the huge house was sold to an Arab family and everyone was happy. So, if like me you still think imperial, beware metrication.

When moving abroad we must remember that rules and customs differ very much from those to which we are accustomed. Wills, taxes, pensions, laws, medical arrangements and so on must be considered. Every country is different, and of course, so are the languages spoken. Here are a few reminders of the less glamorous but essential matters for consideration when moving abroad.

'So you think you speak English?'

Not only the English speak English. There are some 400 million people who would say that their language was English, but their day-to-day conversation is often as different as a Londoner's is from that of a Geordie. The written word can be equally confusing. In America, for instance, the ground floor, as we call it, is referred to as the first floor. A plot is called a lot, curtains become drapes, baths rather engagingly are called tubs, and a wardrobe is a closet. Beware of words like 'lot-line' which means boundary, and duplex which is another word for semi-detached house. As for the privy, well, any number of euphemisms are used in America, including the bathroom, the commode, and my favourite, the rest room.

Vocabulary can cause misunderstandings: 'breaker box' is not something fighters do, but a fuse box. A 'spigott in the yard' is a water tap in the garden. That specialist lawyer you engage will understand the local lingo which is a very important necessity.

The search

The primary reason for conducting a search is to establish title to your chosen property, but ownership is not the only consideration. Your solicitor will also be expected to make certain that the buildings included in the sale were built with the knowledge and approval of the local authority. If what you are buying is no more than a piece of land, then there will be a limit on the percentage of the land you may cover with a building, if indeed permission exists for any building at all. This percentage could vary according to the location; in Spain, for instance, a different set of rules applies for an ordinary building plot for a *finca urbana* from those where a rural *finca rustica* is proposed.

Should the property you wish to purchase be an already established villa or apartment, then do check that there are no outstanding debts assigned against it. If there are, then in Spain those debts pass on to you once you have purchased the property.

Since location and environment are the basic reasons for the proposed purchase in the first place, it is vital that no stone is left unturned during the search even if it costs a little more (about one and a half to two per cent of the purchase price is usually right). Give your lawyer written instructions on what you want him to do. Tell him not to confine himself to the land or property in question, but to the area immediately surrounding your new home. I learned of one very well known British builder recently who moved in to his brand new villa right by the sea only to find that a 12-storey block of flats was about to be built next door, taking all his sunshine. Were I that builder I would sue my lawyer and kick myself hard for not examining the area plans at the local town hall myself. There is really no substitute for a personal check of this kind.

Seeking compensation from a lawyer is not easy, especially in a foreign country. They all tend to close ranks when one of their number is being got at. The most satisfactory legal arrangement of all is the instruction of an expert firm in Great Britain who will then instruct a local lawyer to carry out the search. Then, in the unlikely event of any claim for compensation you at least know that the lawyer has professional indemnity insurance covering negligence. Finding the right lawyer should not be too difficult now that they are allowed to advertise their services. As a start one could ask FOPDAC or ABOPA to send their list of recommended British notaries.

The building

Though consumer protection is beginning to manifest itself in some countries, including Spain, *'Caveat Emptor'* still rules. Get quotes from more than one builder with a good local track record, and be sure to inspect some of their local work and talk to the customers.

Do not let them lay a brick, nor should you spend a single peseta until that all-important title deed is in your hand. Then insist upon paying the builder in stages which should be linked to actual progress in work rather than dates; also, because *mañana* is a fairly ubiquitous word, insist when agreeing the contract that there is a termination date, with penalties for failure to complete the work on time. Finally, it would not be unreasonable on your part to retain a small percentage of the final payment for a few months past the completion date as a guarantee against serious defects. By that I do not mean the more obvious minor problems that always seem to appear in brand new homes, but rather the sort of faults that arise from negligence or incompetence. In some countries, Spain in particular, a guarantee, similar to the 10-year protection scheme of our own National House-Building Council, has been brought in.

Wills

One of the first tasks after the decision to live abroad has been taken concerns the last thing we plan for - death. It is the one event in life that is certain. Rules concerning intestacy vary widely from country to country. Even if you have made a will in the United Kingdom it is absolutely vital that both husband and wife should make new wills in the country in which they plan to live. If they are buying or living in more than one country, then a will under each country's laws should be drawn up.

Many countries practise primogeniture and not the principle of inheritance by the surviving spouse, thus in the case of a man or woman dying intestate, greater shares of the estate might be given to children than to the surviving spouse. Then again, it is not always possible to will one's entire estate to a wife or husband, and certainly not to a cats' home. Laws in some countries are, in some ways, more sensitive than our own.

There are no fewer than 400 articles in the Spanish civil laws of inheritance, all reasonable and humane, but very different from those of Great Britain. In many ways the laws of Mediterranean countries are more compassionate than ours, being family orientated to cover a general lack of faith in standard justice. Woe betide the common law wife, for if she inherits the estate, taxes will take most of it back.

An English will is valid, but the £250 spent on a Spanish will could prove vital to those you leave behind. In the case of intestacy each region of Spain has its own rules, but normally a widow would be allowed to live in the home for the rest of her life and also be entitled to the interest from any investments; she would not be allowed to spend the capital or proceeds from a sale of the house. A widow deciding to leave her property to the cat home would be told that such a will was invalid, and if she proceeded with it members of her family would, if they were sensible, successfully contest it after her death. If during her life she decides to move back to England the children would be expected to pay her the rental income from the house or the interest on the proceeds of its sale.

Inheritance taxes (*impuesto de succesiones*) are assessed according to the beneficiaries' relationship with the deceased. Members of the immediate family - widow, children and parents, pay least, the maximum in the scale of charges being 13 per cent. Uncles and cousins pay rather more, but cat homes (and the like), as well as friends and common law wives, can end up paying as much as 90 per cent.

Do check on the regional differences. In Barcelona, for instance, the first male gets all, though the widow is protected as above. In Madrid, the widow can inherit half the estate while in Marbella a man can leave a third to his wife, a third shared among his children, and a third to the cat home.

However bizarre the wishes of the deceased they will be carried out unless there is an objection, but the court will always support a just claim where family has been disinherited. When children have the harrowing job of dividing up their parents' estate they will normally appear before the local notary to make an inheritance declaration; they will then go to the tax office to negotiate the tax by placing a value on the property and other assets.

If the home is then sold the deeds at the land registry will have an 'embargo preventivo' stamped on them until the outstanding taxes are paid. It is all very fair, and the need to go to court is rare. A little planning can save much distress.

This is a subject to be left to the professionals as are the rules concerning capital transfer tax, which vary from country to country. It may seem a morbid topic during the euphoria of moving to the sun, but plans for death have to be made. In life a man may wish to be in Spain, but in death he may wish to repose in an English country churchyard. The British Consulate will advise on death certificates and transport of a corpse back to England, but they will not pay for it. Provision must be made for this inevitable but we hope distant event.

Health resorts

Some people have allergies, arthritis and other health problems which should be taken into consideration when moving overseas. Three places spring immediately to mind where health is almost assured...Ischia, Lanzarote and part of the Costa Blanca, in Spain.

Property on Ischia is scarce and expensive. I was privileged to stay in a villa beside the gardens belonging to Sir William Walton, and sip wine with him on his beautiful terrace; he loved the island, and benefited greatly from its remarkable climate.

It is not so much the climate that makes this island special, however, but its curious hot springs that bubble from the bowels of the earth; these contain life-enhancing salts which, if we are to believe the claims of the countless baths, cure everything from acne to xenophobia.

Whether the lame can really leap after treatment there I cannot say for certain, but the facilities for care are excellent. One hotel has 10 dialysis machines to augment the remedial and beauty treatments. The salts bubble up from what geologists call the Fields of Phlegethon, but I prefer the ancient Greek name, the Hades River of Fire.

Legend has it that a giant named Typhon flirted with Jupiter's wife; his death sentence was commuted to life entombment beneath Ischia's huge Mount Epomeo, after Venus had interceded on his behalf. The condition of the leniency was that the unhappy Typhon's tears should acquire healing qualities.

Across in mainland Spain there are the salinas, behind bustling Torrevieja, which made the Dead Sea seem normal. I called it the Costa del Efficacio, for even my high jumper's knees stopped creaking after paddling there. The trouble is that it is like bathing in porridge, and one feels a little like Lot's wife afterwards.

A residential and retirement health care resort called Jago Jardin (Garden Lake) could be well worth investigating, both for young and old. Of course you don't have to be ailing to enjoy a holiday there. Tiny units start at £15,000 in price,

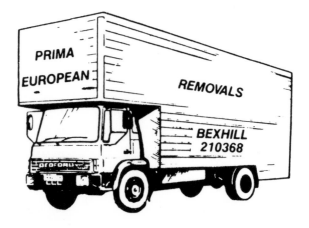

but they really are tiny; better ones cost just over £30,000; they have three bedrooms and a roof terrace.

Lanzarote is well known for its health giving dry climate; people literally feel the aches drain away as they land on the tarmac (see Canary Island section). The omens were not good when I arrived at Club La Santa, a Danish sports and health resort whose stark appearance earned it the name 'Colditz'; in fact the small windows are intended to keep the heat out of the rooms.

It is all a trifle monastic, and beaches are miles away. Although the sea is right next door, the rocks make bathing dangerous. All sports are catered for, and a blonde Aphrodite in a canary yellow tracksuit greets one at the airport; an immediate straightening of the back and tensing of stomach muscles is required. All of Aphrodite's friends were bronzed and fit too, honed on a diet of salads and Scandinavian exercises. I thought I was doing well on the running track until she swept past and inquired: 'Sir, can you tell me the time?'. No 23-year-old calls me 'Sir' and gets away with it — a 55 second lap was called for.

Holidays here are sold on a time-share basis, but for someone wanting to live on Lanzarote there are developments like Playa Bastian which are very suitable (though there are not so many Aphrodites there). A lot of British people do own weeks at Club La Santa, and most were satisfied. Children are always under the eye of the staff, and good wine is available in the supermarket. I thought there were some statues by the pool, but I discovered they were statuesque Mancunian ladies, motionless — 'overdid the aerobics — can't move' they admitted. Get fit before you go, I say.

On the move

If the overseas property you buy is initially no more than a holiday home it will probably be easier to furnish it locally. On the other hand, if it is a villa or apartment in a new development the builder may well offer a choice of furnishing 'packages' which, because of his bulk purchasing power, will certainly be good value. Some of these schemes offer a complete home. If the property is for letting the furnishing should obviously be robust and washable rather than elegant or tinselly. Prized antiques and expensive music centres are an unnecessary additional risk, unless you are filthy rich and adequately insured.

If the new home is for yourself a different set of considerations arises. Leaving these shores can be quite a wrench, as can abandoning the family home... that conker tree planted years ago by one of the children probably means quite a lot to you today. It is bad enough uprooting yourselves without leaving behind the possessions of a lifetime. There are bound to be treasured possessions that most people would want to take with them. Moving them, however far, is a job for the specialists.

One can of course hire a van, load it up, and follow on with the old cock linnet;

but long waits could ensue at some borders if the proper papers have not been completed. Also, the linnet might not be admissible. Better to use the professionals even if the initial cost of the move may seem high, as you will doubtless have enough to worry about without undertaking any more DIY.

Start by contacting the British Association of Removers (BAR), at 279 Gray's Inn Road, London WC1X 8SY which will send you a list of about 80 firms specialising in overseas removals, plus a simple guide to organising a trouble-free move. Having selected a firm, notify them of your date of departure and also stipulate the degree of urgency for delivery to your new home - the latter could greatly influence the mode of transport and route chosen. Make a complete inventory of your home, both for insurance purposes and for Customs declaration. A returnable deposit may be charged to discourage people from trading in furniture, antiques and the like. Special consents may be required for some items: guns and explosives will probably not be permitted to travel with your furniture. Do note that the mildest of video films might prove unacceptable to some countries.

Moving house involves a lot of paperwork, and the more of this which can be handed over to an expert the better. Some items might prove more trouble than they are worth. A television, for instance, will almost certainly require conversion to the new country's system, and the cost may make this impractical.

Similarly, other electrical goods and in most cases gas appliances, are probably better left behind.

Cars are a different matter. It really depends how much of a friend your car is. You might be allowed to keep a car in your new home if it is for use by you as a tourist from time to time, but if it is for regular use at all times then the cost of re-registering it might tilt the balance between keeping it and buying another one in your new country. In Spain, for instance, provided you are there only as a tourist for a maximum of six months, your car can stay with you and you can use it. As a new permanent resident you are allowed the same six months grace but thereafter the full import duty will have to be paid, and this can be quite a lot of money. Anyone maintaining a tourist status in Spain can buy a car there with tourist plates and not have to pay the normal taxes and import duty. But whatever you decide to do, plump for economy, bomb proof suspension and high clearance, rather than luxury - distances and bumps can be great.

Taking the family pet, or even a whole menagerie, is possible in most countries, but it might not be the kindest thing to do. Animals accustomed to our climate might find it difficult to adapt to the relentless sunshine in Cyprus. Quite apart from the journey, the animal may have to endure long quarantine periods, and it will certainly require documentation and health certificates. The Ministry of Agriculture, Fisheries and Food should be approached before any final decision is taken. A pet will almost certainly require a health certificate and proof of at least one inoculation against rabies, perhaps two, as well as an export licence. All this takes time, so if Fido is to go with you to Perth do plan well ahead. Quarantine periods abroad also vary, from nil to six months. If there is the slightest chance of your deciding to return to England remember that your poor pet will then have to sit in a quarantine kennel for a further six months. However, Fido may be an important member of the family in which case, as most European countries do not impose quarantine periods, and provided all the documentation is in order and you are sure he will adapt to his new home, by all means take him along. He will probably integrate with the natives long before you!

The cost of packing the home into a container and taking it abroad is considerable, and since much of the expense is incurred in this country, you will have to pay your chosen removal firm before departure. What if the firm goes bankrupt before or during the move? Provided you have chosen one of the 80 firms listed by the British Association of Removers there will be no problem. The association, through the International Movers Mutual Insurance Company, offers an advance-payment guarantee, so if one of the affiliated companies fails to fulfil its contractual commitment, the association is able to complete the task at no extra cost to the customer.

But how much does all this cost? I asked one of the longest-established firms what they would charge to move an average three bedroom home to three destinations: Sydney in Australia, the south of France, and the south of Spain.

The contents of the home are packed into one of P & O's 20 foot containers, and whilst the first involved a long sea journey, the European destinations were reached by road. The whole operation to the south of France would take up to a week and cost about £2800. The south of Spain would be reached in about the same time but the extra distance would add approximately a further £500 to the cost. Door to door, from your home in England to Sydney, involves a 44-day sea journey, and so the duration of the move would probably be between 8 and 10 weeks. The cost, however, was relatively low - around £1200.

The 'wherewithal'

It is beyond the scope of this book to advise upon pension plans - that would take a book in itself - but moving abroad, especially in retirement, begs certain questions. Is there a double-taxation agreement, for example, and is there a reciprocal agreement between Great Britain and your new country of residence for the drawing of the state pension?

Certainly once the initial payment has been made for the new villa or apartment, local banking arrangements will have to be made to cover day to day expenses. In addition to any long-term investments, a lump sum should be deposited in an easily accessible account for emergencies. Whether or not one should keep a portion of one's estate in Great Britain is up to the individual, but exchange controls could be introduced.

Whatever happens there is no avoiding the payment of tax. If a person is resident for one day more than half a year during the tax year, or if he maintains a property for his own use in Great Britain, he will be expected to pay UK income tax. There is something to be said for the devil you know, for although our taxes are higher than many countries they are not so bad as they once were, and at least the relevant forms are in English.

Living in Spain, or any other foreign country for that matter, could reduce the level of tax if you have a competent guide through the maze. However, a law passed in Spain in December 1983 enabled the 50 administrative provinces to levy a surcharge on income tax at their own discretion. Some have not taken advantage of it whilst others, with high populations of relatively poor people, have grasped the opportunity to put more in the local money box. The tax is not enormous, but it tends to hit more affluent foreigners who have retired to Spain.

People are planning earlier retirements these days, and rightly so; the younger the better. I've always said education is wasted on the young and retirement is wasted on the elderly. But then age is a state of mind, and plenty of young-at-heart octogenarians are living very happily in the sunshine, and drawing their state pension. If you plan to move abroad before reaching your official retirement age (65 for a man and 60 for a woman) it would be wise to preserve your state pension rights by continuing to pay the weekly £3.75 Class III flat rate

A Mortgage Package for a Second Home

If you're planning a second home Hill Samuel provides a really flexible and convenient mortgage package.

■ Advances from £16,000

John G Walker is a Licensed Credit Broker

■ A package that is arranged quickly and professionally

■ One source of contact — your Hill Samuel Investment Services Adviser

■ Full endowment, low-cost endowment, capital repayment or pension linked mortages

■ Life policies arranged through Hill Samuel Life Assurance

■ Competitive interest rates

■ Loan secured by first legal charge over principal residence and assignment of life policy.

For more information, or a written quotation, telephone John G. Walker or complete the coupon below.

Name _____

Address _____

_____ Post Code _____

Telephone (Home) _____ (Business)_____

INVESTMENT SERVICES

John G Walker, FREEPOST,
Hill Samuel Investment Services
Berkeley House, 285 Bath Street
Glasgow G2 4JL
Telephone: 041 204 2501

contribution. Provided this payment continues until qualifying age, you will receive the basic pension wherever you live, but not the earnings related pension which might otherwise be paid. However, not all countries in the world have reciprocal agreements with our government over the payment of the annual cost of living increases and this point should be investigated and considered.

The policy of non-payment of the increase in old-age pensions has been continued by successive governments since 1955, and unfair though it sounds, it could leave a pensioner retiring abroad today, living on the same income in 20 years time. Pensions, insists the government, are designed primarily for people living in this country, and increases, usually in line with the retail price index, reflect the position in Great Britain. People living in Canada, for instance, get the state pension at the rate it was when they moved there, with none of the increases. The argument is that they no longer contribute to indirect taxation by VAT and towards the British economy. Even if the pension is paid into a British bank account and then transferred, the annual increases are not given.

Fortunately, many of the countries normally considered for retirement do have an agreement with the British Government in which cost of living increases are paid, but the exact terms of the agreement may vary. The agreements with Australia and New Zealand mean that the Briton becoming resident there receives the same pension increases as all the other pensioners there. Increases in line with those pensioners living in Great Britain are paid in the following countries: Austria, Belgium, Bermuda, Cyprus, Denmark, Finland, France, West Germany, Gibraltar, Greece, Irish Republic, Israel, Jamaica, Luxembourg, Malta, Mauritius, Netherlands, Portugal, Spain, Switzerland, Turkey, United States and Yugoslavia.

Health matters

Before moving abroad it is worth having a complete check up from your doctor, and also your dentist. Do note that most policies exclude dental treatment from their cover. Also, whilst at the doctor's surgery, check whether any vaccinations are either required or advisable and make sure that any prescribed drugs are admissible in your new country and whether or not they are freely available there.

Although reciprocal national health schemes do exist in certain countries such as Spain, there are some places where the rule 'don't get ill' still applies. Wherever you expect to live, even if you only plan to stay half the year in the United Kingdom and the other half abroad, planning for health care should be an absolute priority. Leaflets are available from the DHSS giving advice on medical treatment abroad; there are other leaflets available from insurance companies on private medical insurance which is also essential, especially if

bought from a UK-based company. There are plenty of schemes available, and the cheapest is not necessarily the best.

Most foreign countries recognise British based medical insurance companies, and generally speaking it is better to buy British. Whichever of the many policies you decide to use it is vital that it covers you for treatment in ANY hospital and with ANY doctor, and in case you decide to opt for treatment back in Britain, the policy should cover the cost of repatriation. Some overseas policies specify the hospitals where treatment must be obtained, but this is not much good if you are taken ill nowhere near one of the named treatment centres!

One scheme worth investigating is Expatriate Assistance, represented in the United Kingdom by Kent Insurance and Securities Services (Overseas), known by the comforting acronym of KISS, and based in Ashford, Kent. The company organises a range of cover with different categories according to the country concerned. Area A, for instance, includes much of Europe but excludes the USA and Canada, with a limit of £5000 cover.

Bearing in mind how costly medical treatment can be I would go for one of the more comprehensive schemes offered by KISS, with cover up to at least £10,000 a year, preferably £20,000, and a daily limit of about £150. But there are certain exclusion clauses which should be noted. For instance, you are not covered for dentistry or childbirth, nor for accidents occurring whilst under the influence of drugs or alcohol or while participating in hazardous sports. Hazardous sports include mountaineering, hang-gliding and deep-sea diving, as well as competitive horse-riding and motor-cycle racing. Squash, cricket and scuba diving are all right, as are non-competitive horse-riding and motor-cycling. The cover offered in this policy does not cover illness or injury caused by a declared epidemic or war, even civil war, nor are radiation poison or geriatric care included. That still leaves plenty of illnesses you can have where treatment will be paid for, and in most cases presentation of the insurance card will be all that is necessary. The hospital or doctor should then send the account to your insurers.

The sooner you take out the insurance the better, for some companies have a maximum age limit at which cover can start and others charge more for people who join schemes after the age of 65.

One of the best all-round covers is offered by The Exeter Hospital Aid Society, 5/7 Palace Gate, Exeter, which has been offering medical insurance to expatriates for over 20 years and now has policy holders in more than 100 countries worldwide. The scheme involves the payment of an annual premium that is the same whatever your age, but there is a joining premium calculated on a sliding scale for people above normal retirement age. This premium can be considerable, approaching £900 if you leave it until you are three score years and ten, but remember this is a once-only payment. Once in the scheme, an annual payment of £351 would probably be sufficient cover for a couple living in Spain. They could spend more, but this sum should be enough to cover all hospital and surgeon's fees. There is no overall maximum limit on the fees covered each year. Some members of the scheme also take advantage of the society's general practice cover; for an additional £28 a year the couple would be able to reclaim at least some of the doctor's fees and the drugs he prescribes. As with the KISS scheme the policy does not include cover for existing illness or physical condition. However there are fewer exclusion clauses...if you fall downstairs after a long communion with Rioja or topple off the side of a mountain, Exeter Hospital Aid will pay for you to be put together again. However, remember that some well-known private medical schemes will expect you to have been a member for some time if you suddenly require cover overseas. The two I have mentioned here have no such requirement.

Insurance

This is another area where rules vary widely from country to country. As with all insurance you get only what you pay for; for your home, its contents, your car, and of great importance, your personal liability. As far as the car is concerned third-party cover is essential and compulsory. In Spain insurance rates for cars are state controlled, so that even if you use a British company based in Spain the premiums will be the same as those charged by a Spanish company.

It will probably be necessary to insure your house and its contents with a local company, but your existing English-based company may well have a subsidiary at or close to your new home. Make an inventory of everything you want covered, plus its value, and remember to revise the valuation regularly.

As with estate agents, lawyers, removal firms and so on, it is essential to avoid what are now called 'cowboys'. In Spain proper insurance agents will be able to show you an identity card, containing a photograph, to prove they are an *agent colegiado*, that is to say a member of the College of Agents. He will naturally try to sell you as much insurance as you can afford, but on the other hand if you decide to gamble and insist on minimal cover it is no good complaining when you find your home burgled. If you are not going to be resident at the property all the year round your insurance premiums should be paid by a standing order at your bank - in this way they will not be forgotten.

One London-based firm that specialises in insurance of holiday homes abroad is Andrew Copeland at 230 Portland Road (01 656 2544). The firm offers cover underwritten at Lloyds which is more or less in line with the cost of insurance in the United Kingdom. The premium rates are £1.75 per £1000 for buildings; £6.25 per £1000 for contents; and £25 per £1000 for special items. The bulk of the company's business is in Spain, Portugal, Italy, and also France, where premiums are slightly higher. The plan offers cover against fire, lightning, earthquakes (important in parts of Portugal), burst pipes, floods, riot damage, theft, and public liability, amongst other things. Excluded from the policy is any cover against sequestration, but for about another £5 per £1000 this can be arranged - a policy for the real pessimist! Unlike most companies their policies do not exclude periods when the property is not occupied.

If you are a permanent resident in a foreign country such as Spain, where cover is supposed to be organised by a Spanish-based company, Copeland can continue to arrange the insurance provided the home-owner maintains an external bank account from which to pay the premiums.

Other financial arrangements

Most readers, I suspect, will have already decided how to pay for their overseas retirement or holiday home. Letting the property might help offset some of the cost, but it will not cover all mortgage repayments. In the past most Britons who needed mortgage facilities raised money on the security of their home in England; overseas banks did and do offer loans, but the process can be complicated, with the buyer rarely being able to borrow more than 50 per cent of the purchase price.

On the subject of banking, a Briton living in Spain as a resident is obliged to bank in pesetas, and interest rates for deposits are much lower than those for non-residents who can bank there in sterling or other foreign currencies.

If you are moving abroad on a permanent basis to avoid Britain's high taxation by becoming a non-resident (i.e. you are to be 'domiciled' in a foreign country, as opposed to being simply resident), you will not be allowed to own a residence in Great Britain. Paradoxically you may retain property that is a commercial venture, such as a block of income-producing flats. However, if considering overseas loans, do think carefully about the repayments and currency exchange as the latter can make the loans considerably more expensive.

Letting your second home

If the prime purpose of your villa is for your own use and for eventual retirement, its letting potential may not be too important. Either way it is important to go for the best location you can find. Unfortunately, even if you check and double-check that your outlook is protected because it is a Green Zone, buildings can suddenly erupt almost overnight. Local authorities have a nasty habit in a few areas of 're-zoning'. Check on the building record held by the local authority.

If your new home is to earn its keep, 'wash its face' as estate agents say, it is important to tell your agent this, for it could influence the choice of property. Some developments are very much better geared for holiday letting than others. Some developers offer a guaranteed income from your flat, but I am nervous of such promises unless they are on a year to year basis. Anyway, the guarantee would probably have to be lower than the unit's real potential.

About the best net annual return you could hope to achieve in Spain's Costa del Sol would be 10 per cent of the purchase price, but a more realistic average would probably be 5 per cent. People who bought at Bena Vista near Marbella, which is fully geared for holiday letting, have received a net income, after deduction of all charges, of close to 10 per cent. Not far away a very 'up-market' development called Jardines de las Golondrinas (Garden of the Swallows), with its high charges, shows at best about 5 per cent return. However, while the first development shows good capital growth it is nowhere near as high as the 64 per cent rise in price over two years of a two bedroom apartment at the second development.

If no letting facility exists at your development then it is important to use a reputable agent if you propose getting an income from your home. Bear in mind the risk of not being able to rid yourself of a tenant - be certain that the unit is let only for holidays.

In certain countries a landlord might also be held responsible for the iniquities of his tenants. A good management company will retain a 'dilapidation' deposit, in case of damage during the tenancy. This, of course, is refundable at the end of the tenancy if all is well.

Returning to the UK

Suppose you find that it was all a terrible mistake; you are bored, fed up with sunshine and cocktail parties, run out of hobbies, and generally yearn for the old motherland. Is the whole process easily reversible? How do you go about doing it? For the most part, returning to the United Kingdom is the reverse of organising your move abroad. However, two very important elements always arise, repatriation of money and the selling of your overseas home.

Provided you have made your monetary arrangements correctly there should be no problems. The biggest fear is that your worldly wealth could be locked up in a country you have grown to dislike. In some countries there could be a problem getting your money out (Greece springs to mind) but these are exceptions; there could, however, be delays in its repatriation. Most countries allow you to repatriate what you have brought in, provided it was correctly transferred and you have bank certificates or the like to prove it. They should also allow the release of any reasonable profits made by your account but do bear in mind the current state of the currency market. As with the changing of pounds sterling into US dollars or pesetas into pounds, a loss or a gain can arise when currency changes occur.

Every country has its own rules, which is why we now begin our gentle voyage to some of the most likely ports for investment. As far as selling is concerned, if you were satisfied with the agent through whom you bought, at least give him a crack at selling for you, and do take his advice on valuation. The doctor or the vicar might think your home is worth more, but generally speaking the agent has his finger on the pulse of the property market. Selling abroad can be expensive and we have been spoiled by agents' fees in the UK. In Portugal the average fee is around six per cent, while in Spain it can be eight to ten per cent, even as high as fifteen per cent. This is because of the wide range of prices in Spain. An agent has to do as much work to sell a £12,000 studio in the Costa Blanca as he does to sell a millionaire's penthouse in Marbella. He also has to share his commission with his British associate, for the property would almost certainly be marketed abroad, rather than in Spain.

But best of all, before you buy find somewhere you like and feel you could enjoy. How awful to wish you had stayed put, and spend your declining years musing on what might have been.

PART II

Andorra

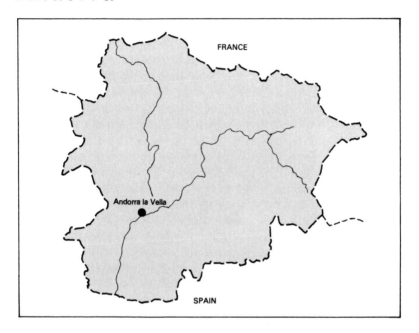

Status: Co-principality
Currency: French franc/peseta
Capital: Andorra la Vella
Area: 465 sq km (180 sq miles)
Population: 43,000
Language: Catalan
Longitude: 0° E   **Latitude**: 43° N
Average temperature: High 26° C (79° F) Low -7° C (18° F)
Annual average rainfall: 1200mm (47in)
Contact: The Andorran Delegation, 63 Westover Road, London SW18 2RF
(01 874 8406)

Nestling in the Pyrenées, about the size of the Isle of Wight, is Andorra, a
country of some 43,000 people whose homes are all higher than Snowdon and
whose quality of life is high, like the mountains topped with 'icing sugar' which
surround this land-locked 'island'. Like Switzerland, Andorra has remained neu-

47

tral, and it is a tax haven second to none. Indeed there is no personal taxation whatsoever, the country's income arising chiefly from a small import duty levied on all goods coming in.

Until recently it was Andorra's inaccessibility that added to its charm; the very journey prompted several books. Now there is the trans-Pyrenean highway, linking Toulouse and Barcelona, with Andorra la Vella - the highest capital in Europe - only about 25 miles from it, through the new Cadi tunnel. (Vella does not mean old, but is derived from an ancient word meaning city.) Coupled with this fast motor route there is now a small airport just over the border in Spain, at Seo d'Urgell which it is hoped will be operational in time for the 1992 Olympic Games water sports here. With about 65 peaks soaring above 10,000 feet, the flight can be both breath-taking and heart-stopping.

There are few places in the world more beautiful than Andorra in spring, and if you are late for spring all you have to do is climb another 1000 feet to find it. Carpets of gentians, orchids, meadow sweet and azaleas, and of course the national flower, the pheasant's eye narcissus (*Narcissus poeticus*), which the locals call *grandalla*, spread before a walker. Rushing mountain streams and a massed choir of insects complete the welcome.

The cost of living in Andorra is remarkably low, and there is not even capital gains tax if you decide eventually to sell your home. Strikes are illegal; unemployment is practically non-existent, and that is the way the Andorrans want to keep it so work permits remain hard to come by. Since it is on the same latitude as Rome it can get pretty warm during the summer months, but in the winter one is glad of the open fires which most houses, even new ones, retain; one ton of oak logs costs about £60. Even during the tourist season the crime rate is low, so the little country employs only 60 policemen. It has no army, nor any diplomats.

Andorra enjoys the protection of two 'princes', the Spanish Bishop of Urgel and the French President, but it remains an independent republic - its boundaries and identity surviving a millenium of European history. It is reported that a consortium of Arabs once tried to buy the country, but its residents consider it beyond price.

The country was originally divided into six parishes, one for each of the petals on the national flower. Today however there are seven, despite the fact that the flower has shown no signs yet of growing another petal! Each parish elects four councillors who serve on the Consell de las Valls (the Council General of the Valleys). It is clearly accepted that they are there to serve and protect the people of Andorra. Ask anyone there who is his sovereign and he will answer 'The People'. It is an irresistible place. The sea is 100 miles away, but the country's lakes are well stocked with trout. Nearly everything, including power, is cheap, and in all directions there are the mountains, ever changing in appearance, but ever beautiful.

Buying a property here should not be difficult; indeed of the 43,000 or so residents only 12,000 are truly Andorran. There are about 20,000 Spaniards, 8000 French and 3000 other nationalities, of which approximately 1000 are British. The main language is Catalan, but Spanish, French, and sometimes a little English is normally understood. If the property is for permanent occupation, the authorities will require evidence of ownership, or tenancy, a bank reference proving solvency and a character reference to show you have no criminal record. For a retired couple moving to Andorra there should be no problems, other than a bit of a wait (perhaps a year), provided they do not intend to seek any employment. Anyway, who needs employment with all those mountains to climb?

The capital, Andorra la Vella, can be a bustling and crowded place, especially at the height of the tourist season, but it is worth a visit for its shops and historic buildings. Away from the town, the villages and smaller towns are remarkably quiet and peaceful. A few years ago a German company built a grotesque block of flats on a beautiful hillside, but out of folly came order. Now the authorities keep a strict control on the types of building and building materials used. The mountainous terrain means that about 90 per cent of the land area is unusable, other than for brave ski fanatics. The land that is available for agriculture and building is therefore at a premium, rising considerably in value every year.

A few years ago it was possible to find one of the old barns (*bordas*) to restore, but these have nearly all now been discovered, and they can command high prices. A *borda* conversion will probably set you back £130,000 or more, as indeed could a large detached home.

Most people are settling for a modern apartment in a traditional-styled block, with a balcony and all the comfort and convenience of twentieth-century building. A studio can still be found for as little as £25,000. Two and three bedroom apartments can usually be found for between £45,000 and £60,000, but in the capital some of the larger apartments can cost a lot more, up to £150,000 or more.

Although Andorra is so admirably suited to those seeking the quieter and more relaxed style of living, there is no doubt that it is appealing more and more to active holiday makers. In addition to the rapidly expanding ski-ing facilities, there is a magnificent new sports complex and adjacent apartment block at La Massana, not far from the capital. More than 50 studios, one and two bedroom flats are being sold, some on an aparthotel basis, with prices starting at £44,000. The sports facilities include seven glass-backed championship squash courts, four tennis courts, two of them covered, a large swimming pool, shooting gallery, gymnasium, plus restaurants and bars to re-charge the batteries. New developments close to the Arinsal ski lifts include one called Prats Sobirans, now sold out, and Amadeus where 1, 2 and 3 bedroom flats can still be found from about £36,000.

Buying procedures are said to be among the simplest and least hazardous in Europe. However the buyer is obliged to use a local lawyer, some of whom do speak English, if he wants legal assistance. Most property is sold freehold, and normally both buyer and seller appear before one of the two notaries, after which the buyer receives his *Escriptura Publica*. If a mortgage is involved the bank may also be represented. It all costs very little, about half of one per cent for the notary's fee and a small charge is made by the estate agent (*gestoria*) for processing all the paper work. When buying an apartment in a new block the *escriptura* will only be issued when all the work is finished. Meanwhile the buyer receives a private contract drawn up by a lawyer or, to be absolutely safe, he can meet the notary and ask for an *escriptura privada*. Developers seldom offer any insurance-backed guarantee of completion, but a buyer can obtain a bank guarantee at his own expense, costing about £200. Local finance can normally be arranged, in a choice of currencies (Swiss francs are best at present) and there is no financial penalty in the event of an early repayment of the mortgage. With new buildings, payment is normally made in three stages, one-third on signing the purchase contract, one-third when the roof is finished, and a final one-third when the keys are handed over.

It all sounds too good to be true. So what are the snags? The very cheapness of the best wines and spirits are a hazard in themselves, and on long winter evenings the coveting of neighbours' wives (or husbands) is another.

Anguilla

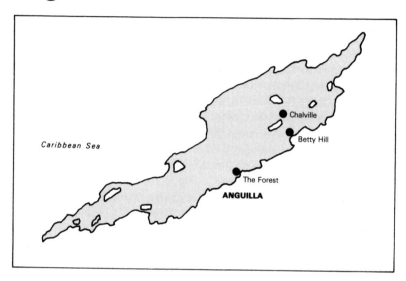

Status: British Dependent Territory
Currency: East Caribbean dollar
Capital: The Valley
Area: 9 sq km (36 sq miles)
Population: 7700 (1982)
Language: English
Longitude: 63° W   **Latitude**: 18° N
Average temperature: 27° C (81° F)
Annual average rainfall: 1300 mm (51 in)
Contact: The Foreign and Commonwealth Office, Whitehall, London
(01 233 3000)

This long, narrow island is 16 miles by 3 miles, but despite its size the standard of housing is amongst the highest in the Caribbean.

Buyers must first obtain an alien's land holding licence and the stamp duty at purchase is only one per cent. The tourist potential is being developed on this island but it has still retained its charm.

Anguilla has a rather dry climate, and about 30 white coral sand beaches. Neither the soil nor the weather make the flat island conducive to intensive agricultural development. People lucky enough to live here are charged an annual property tax based on three per cent of the estimated annual rental value of their home.

St Kitts and Nevis

As sugar production makes way for tourism, access to many islands is improving, and St Kitts and its unspoilt neighbour Nevis are no exception. Property prices are high, few houses being available under 150,000 US dollars. Stamp duty is normally four per cent, two per cent each paid by vendor and buyer. A 10 per cent tax is charged on property purchased by aliens except when they are buying in Frigate Bay itself. An annual house tax is levied, based on five per cent of the estimated annual rental value, but there is no personal income tax of offshore income. There is a small government backed title insurance of less than 0.5 per cent of the property's value. Residential status on the islands is possible, but a fee of about 600 US dollars is charged at the initial stage.

Antigua and Barbuda

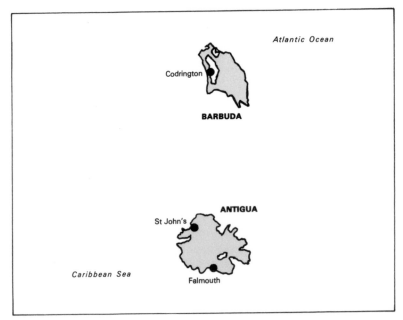

Status: Independent State
Currency: East Caribbean dollar
Capital: St John's
Area: 442 sq km (179 sq miles) total of both islands

Population: 76,500 (1981)
Language: English
Longitude: 62°W   **Latitude**: 17°N
Average temperature: 27°C (81°F)
Annual average rainfall: 1020 mm (40 in)
International airport: Coolidge International Airport (Antigua)
Contact: The High Commission of Antigua and Barbuda, 15 Thayer Street, London W1 (01 486 7073)

Antigua and Barbuda are part of the Leeward chain of islands, with Antigua being far the larger and more populated of the two. Their physical appearance is also quite different. Barbuda is flat, the highest point only 44m (145 feet) high, and the land is covered with scrub bushes and dry, wild grasses. Antigua, not the most lush of the Caribbean islands, does sport a more attractive landscape. Antigua is 279 sq km (108 sq miles) in area and Barbuda some 161 sq km (62 sq miles). Tourism employs 60 per cent of the population and accounts for over half of the islands' income.

Travel between the two islands is easy with a 10-minute plane ride covering the 40 km (25 mile) distance. Barbuda's capital, Codrington, was named after the man who used to own the island, and before the emancipation of slaves, Barbuda used to be a slave colony.

People wanting to buy property on either island must first apply to the Ministry of Agriculture in St John's, the capital of Antigua. This would normally be through a local solicitor: a list of solicitors and estate agents can be obtained through the islands' High Commission.

Once an alien land holder's permit has been obtained, a 10 per cent property tax is charged on any property bought. Provided the applicant can show proof of good character and adequate financial means, there should not be any problems in getting the necessary consent. A small land tax is charged annually but this is only 70p for every acre owned. There is no other tax as such but services such as water and electricity are paid for separately; this is common to most of the islands in the Caribbean.

In addition to some interesting housing developments which are appealing to a number of US as well as British buyers, there are also some attractive time-sharing opportunities. If and when the time comes to sell, there are no restrictions on the moving of funds and there is no capital gains tax either. A large house with an acre of garden could be built for £50,000.

Australia

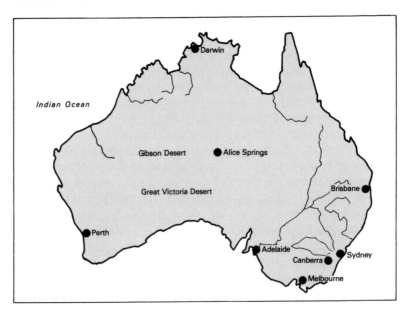

Status: Independent State
Currency: Australian dollar
Capital: Canberra
Area: 7,686,884 sq km (2,967,909 sq miles)
Population: 14,927,000 (1981)
Language: English
Longitude: Between 113° and 153° E
Latitude: Between 10° and 43° S
Average temperature: Varied, dependent on location
Annual average rainfall: Varied
International airport(s): 6; including Sydney, Melbourne and Perth
Contact: The Australian High Commission, Australia House, The Strand,
London WC2B 4LA (01 379 4334)

Some people go to the other end of the world for their retirement, but despite
its vast size, entry into Australia is no longer as easy as it was. More people want
to go there, it seems, than Australia is now prepared to allow. Anyone wanting
to live and work there is expected to have expertise or a talent which is going
to benefit his new hosts; alternatively there must be a close relative who will

54

sponsor him. This does not mean that someone contemplating retirement there will automatically be disqualified if he has no relatives in the country. People of retirement age, which is the same as that in the UK, can apply for permission to retire to Australia provided they have good character references and are in good health. There are, however, fairly strict financial requirements. Applicants must be at least 55 years old and have either: (1) $A500,000 for transfer or (2) $A150,000 for establishment costs, plus pension or additional capital to provide an annual income of at least $A35,000 ($A30,000 for a single person).

Those fortunate enough to qualify will enjoy one of the highest living standards in the world, and wonderful weather. No wonder they drink so much amber nectar and play such good tennis. Buying property involves much the same disciplines as in England, but legal and conveyancing charges do vary slightly from state to state. Generally speaking, they should certainly not amount to more than 10 per cent of the purchase price.

As in England there is also a wide range of property and prices. Sydney has some of the most expensive houses, averaging around £60,000 for a three bedroom detached home. Although there are now some apartment blocks and town houses, the typical Australian house remains the single storey dwelling on a large plot of up to a quarter of an acre. Taking the three bedroom detached house as an example, the same home in Canberra would cost £50,000; in Melbourne £45,000; in Adelaide £42,000; and in Perth it would cost £40,000. There is also a range of property on the cooler island of Tasmania. Hobart houses of the same size might cost £38,000.

Moving funds to Australia is uncomplicated, and at present there is no capital gains tax on resales. This could change soon, for the tax systems are being reviewed. However, once embraced by warm Australian weather not many people would be in a hurry to leave it.

The Bahamas

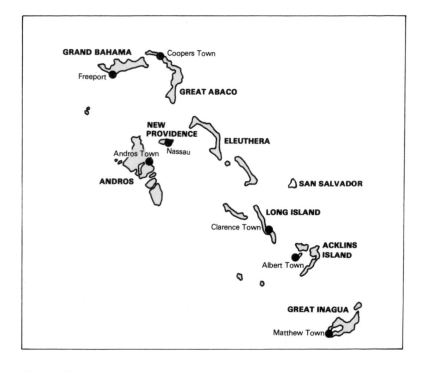

Status: Independent State
Currency: Bahamian dollar
Capital: Nassau
Area: 11,406 sq km (4404 sq miles)
Population: 238,000
Language: English
Longitude: 72°W **Latitude**: 21°N
Average temperature: 26.1°C (79°F)
Annual average rainfall: 850 mm (33 in)
International airport(s): 2; Nassau, Freeport
Contact: The Bahamas High Commission, 10 Chesterfield Street,
London W1X 8AH (01 408 4488)

There are considerable tax benefits for people living on the Bahamas, but the high humidity between June and November might persuade many that summer in Britain might be best, with winter spent on one of these admirable islands. On these many islands there are plenty of sophisticated developments, with golf courses and other essentials but also plenty of unspoilt territory. As with Florida which is directly across the Florida Straits, adequate medical insurance is absolutely vital.

Anyone wishing to live there for more than eight months in a year needs to apply to the Director of Immigration at PO Box N-831 in Nassau, where each case is considered on its merits. Financial security will be needed, but there is no hard and fast rule on the required minimum income. There is an annual fee of B$1000 with a further 20 dollars for each dependant. However someone seeking permanent resident status (and this can be easier for a Briton than it is for an American) will pay a once-only permit fee of B$5000.

Property is not cheap - indeed close to Nassau it is probably much the same price as it is in the more expensive parts of Florida. But there are 700 beautiful islands to explore, only 30 of which are inhabited. Cheaper property can, of course, be found on some of the less fashionable islands. Once you have found your own favourite an application will have to be made to the Foreign Investment Board in Nassau for the go-ahead to buy. This is to discourage speculation.

Barbados

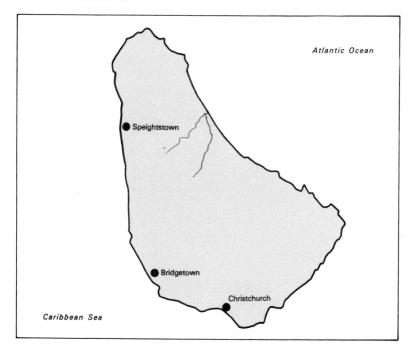

Status: Independent State
Currency: Barbados dollar
Capital: Bridgetown
Area: 430 sq km (166 sq miles)
Population: 260,000 (1979)
Language: English
Longitude: 59° W **Latitude**: 13° N
Average temperature: 26° C (79° F)
Annual average rainfall: 1651 mm (65 in)
International airport: Grantley Adams International Airport
Contact: The Barbados High Commission, 6 Upper Belgrave Street,
London SW1X 8AZ (01 235 8686/9)

The 430 sq km (166 sq miles) of Barbados is largely covered with whispering sugar cane. It is a well organised, highly civilised and manicured island; popular with Britons for many years. The very names of its villages make the 'expat' feel at home - Brighton, Worthing, Hastings, and so on. There is even a Nelson's Column and a Trafalgar Square. The capital, Bridgetown, is a bustling place, with some of the best live-jazz clubs to be found anywhere in the world. Barbadians also live in the Caribbean's most politically stable place, governed by the third oldest democracy in the Commonwealth: the first parliament sat there in 1639.

Americans were prominent in the house buying scene, but they have not swamped this traditionally British market; indeed the strength of the pound has produced a rush of British investment during 1988. There remains a core of long-established British families, many of whom bought land by the coral beaches just after the war and built opulent houses which would now command fairly opulent prices. In fact house prices on Barbados had been static in recent years, but estate agents there are now reporting a seller's market - one could almost say they were snowed under. The government, while still opposed to speculators, is anxious to attract serious investment. However a property transfer tax is imposed on non-nationals both when buying and selling, amounting in total to around 18 per cent (ten per cent at purchase and eight per cent when selling).

Prices on Barbados are usually quoted in US dollars, rather than in sterling or in Barbados dollars. It is possible to spend a million pounds or more on one of the grand beach-side homes, but this would command a daily rent of around £500 at least. Not that this would be all profit, however; such a rent would obtain the tenant a staff including a butler, cook, housekeeper, maid, laundress, gardener and watchman. One long-time resident there told me that his temporary neighbours were a young couple named Mr and Mrs Paul McCartney, but he had no idea what line of business they were in! You can live in a world all of your own in the Caribbean.

The east and west sides of this island are very different from each other. Much as I love the west coast with its coral reefs (the diving is good) the rugged east coast, shaped by the mighty Atlantic, is the more beautiful, with very little development.

There is nothing to stop outsiders buying cheaper property, and indeed there are some very acceptable developments a little way inland where prices are very much more attractive. There is Sunset Crest, in St James, providing a variety of units that are not only ideal for holiday but which have become permanent home for some retired couples from Britain and America. I last visited the development in March 1983, but nearly five years later, the prices had changed very little. A three bedroom villa, fully furnished, can be bought for about US$70,000, while a one bedroom apartment can be found for US$25,000. So you do not have to be a millionaire to retire to Barbados. Points to watch for are the tax liability on rental return, which is quite steep, and possible delays in the repatriation of all the profit from a sale. You are allowed to take out what you brought in together with what the government calls 'a reasonable profit'.

One of the most popular developments has the most awful name, Glitter Bay. The developers admit they were stuck with it, for that is what Mr George Manning called it when he discovered the bay in 1898. The 4 hectares (10 acres) of gardens were planted by the original owner, Sir Edward Cunard, and his Venetian-style mansion has been retained. Although consent exists for 142 units only about half are to be built for fear of devaluing the superb environment. I rather enjoyed being lulled to sleep by a chorus of whistling frogs and crickets, accompanied by the gentle ocean, and woken by wood-doves and 'grackles' (American blackbirds) serenading one another.

Fruit is not so prolific as one might expect on this limestone and coral island, but frangipani and flamboyant trees grow in abundance. The rain, which falls mainly between June and November, percolates rapidly through the limestone, so there are no surface rivers. Below ground there is a fascinating cave landscape of lakes and streams which provide the island with excellent drinking water.

This most easterly of the Lesser Antilles is no tax haven; it has no tropical rain forests, or parrots, but it does offer a sophisticated life style for Britons who can afford it.

Bermuda

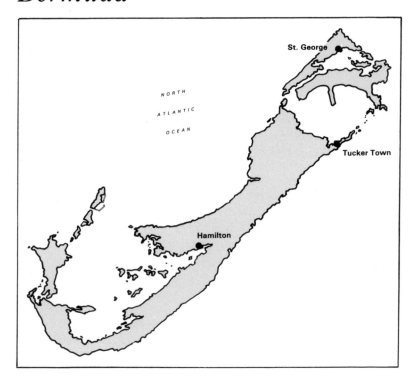

Status: Parliamentary British Colony
Currency: Bermuda dollar
Capital: Hamilton
Area: 53.85 sq km (20.8 sq miles)
Population: 61,000 (1981)
Language: English
Longitude: 64°W **Latitude**: 32°N
Average temperature: 23°C (73°F)
Annual average rainfall: 1463 mm (60 in)
International airport: Kindley Field, St David's Island
Contact: Bermuda Tourism, 6 Burnsall Street, London SW3 3ST (01 734 8813)

A lusty infant name Neville who weighed in at King Edward Hospital, Paget, early in the morning, was, by local standards, born into a poor family; but he had something that millionaires cannot buy - citizenship of Bermuda. Not that residents of this fortunate group of islands cannot welcome new settlers, but as one local estate agent put it: 'They must be good, clean living and upright people'. They must also be extremely wealthy, for to protect young Neville's birthright, only the most expensive houses can be bought by foreigners. An application for citizenship can take a very long time. It is not just for its climate, or its sub-tropical gardens and famous golf courses that the wealthy go to Bermuda; the archipelago is a tax haven. You keep what you earn, and there is no capital gains tax.

Everyone has heard of Bermuda - it is Britain's oldest colony - but many believe it to be in the Caribbean. It is actually further north than the Canary Islands, but because of the warm embrace of the Gulf Stream has a sub-tropical climate. There are more than 150 islands, many of which are uninhabited, and most are bordered by coral reefs that many ancient sailors discovered to their cost. Shakespeare's *Tempest* was inspired by Admiral Somers and his ship, the Sea Venture. The sea bed around Bermuda's 20 sq mile land area is littered with wrecks, as a diving expedition from the excellent but expensive Sonesta Beach Hotel will reveal.

Bermuda is a manicured paradise which attracts nearly half a million tourists every year, 90 per cent of them from the United States. American dollars and dialect have virtually conquered the island since people went there in search of whisky during their prohibition era. The strength of the pound against the dollar has encouraged more British visitors in the last year or so. More Europeans are also being wooed.

The very first visitors arrived there by accident. A Spaniard, Juan de Bermudez, bumped into the reefs early in the sixteenth century, leaving his name for future generations to use. Later Admiral George Somers had similar misfortune on his way with relief supplies for a new American colony. He too gave his name to the islands for a while, but Somers' Islands are now universally known as Bermuda. Bermuda's history is one of swashbuckling heroes and pirates, the Gibraltar of the west!

Despite the number of Americans who live in Bermuda, much is still British. Cars drive on the left, though only residents are allowed to own one, and even that cannot exceed 166 inches in length. There is also a most civilised and rigorously enforced speed limit of 20 mph. Policemen directing traffic in Hamilton, the capital, differ only slightly from London 'bobbies'; a regulation six inches of knee is revealed between stocking tops and neatly pressed Bermuda shorts.

Bermuda has very little crime; guns are illegal, and capital punishment is retained. The last hanging took place less than a decade ago. There is hardly any unemployment, but then there is no unemployment benefit. Many working class people have more than one job, for even though locals can buy the cheaper houses, the cost of living is high.

Although John Lennon is said to have written some of his songs on the island, it is not generally regarded as conducive to creativity. Most people insist on leaving the island at least once a year, otherwise they become what local people call 'rock happy', a sort of self-contentment that sounds not at all unpleasat.

Buying property on the islands is expensive for two reasons. The houses themselves are expensive, and the government demands a 10 per cent property tax on top. An application for a licence to own property usually takes three or four months, and no foreigner can own more than one home there. The two-tier property system was established to protect the less fortunate of the 57,000 residents, 60 per cent of African descent, and operates on a notional rental value that is placed upon each house. No house with an annual rental value (ARV) below BE$40,000 or apartment below BE$15,000 can be bought by foreigners. This effectively rules out the purchase of any house below the value of BE$750,000 or apartment or town house worth less than BE$200,000.

Most houses on Bermuda are known by a name, 'Backgammon', 'Amber', even 'Charleston', and most taxi drivers, who double as tourist guides, know most of the houses. The most prized attribute of a house is a view of the remarkably blue sea, and the price usually reflects this. Whilst most property is in the millionaire bracket there are some town house developments closer to the BE$200,000 minimum. All property is subject to a land tax, similar to our rates, and this averages about BE$2000 per year. All houses, whether large or small, have one thing in common. Roofs are built of coral slates bedded in cement and coated with lime to catch the ample rainfall and channel it into a large reservoir underneath the property. Each home must be self-sufficient for water.

Together with the high cost of living there is a lifestyle, for the wealthy at least, of relaxed formality. Dress ethics are strictly observed - no open-neck shirts in the evening, no topless cycling (even for men), and definitely no hair-curlers outside the privacy of the home for the ladies. There are an awful lot of rules on Bermuda, but sticking to them seems to come naturally.

British Virgin Islands

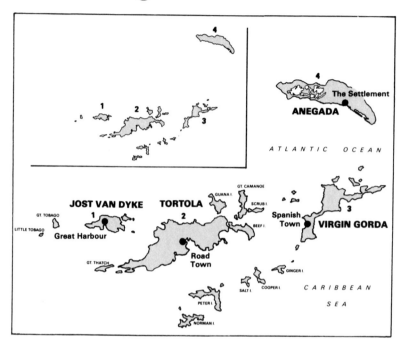

Status: British Dependent Territories
Currency: US dollars
Capital: Road Town
Area: 153 sq km (59 sq miles)
Population: 11,558 (1983)
Language: English
Longitude: 64° W **Latitude**: 18° N
Average temperature: 26.5° C (80° F)
Annual average rainfall: 1000 mm (40 in)
Contact: The West Indian Committee, Albermarle Road, London W1X 4AR
(01 629 6355)

Discovered by Columbus in 1493 and named after St Ursula and her 11,000 virgins, this, like the Cayman Islands, plus the Turks and Caicos Islands, was for years the haunt of pirates and buccaneers. Robert Louis Stevenson's *Treasure Island* is said to be Norman Island though the two main islands are Tortola and Virgin Gorda. Only 15 of the group of 40 islands and islets are actually inhabited.

There may be buried treasure still to be found, but many people buying property here are actually trying to preserve the 'treasure' they have already acquired. There is no wealth tax, death duties, or capital gains tax on these islands. Income tax is charged on income held by individuals in accounts worldwide and is on a sliding scale between five and twenty per cent.

Though there is not a two-tier system of housing, there is also not a lot of scope for good housing below a price of about US$150,000, most modern houses costing above US$200,000. There is an eight per cent stamp duty on purchase and a further one per cent should be allowed for legal charges. Repatriation of funds presents no problem, and there is no exchange control.

'Non-belongers', as the islanders call aliens, must apply for a land holding licence prior to purchase, and you will need financial and character references showing solvency and a clean police record. To avoid excessive speculation in property, the authorities insist that anyone buying land on the islands must develop it within two years of purchase. There is a land tax of US$20 a year for the first acre owned, with a further US$10 for subsequent acres. The house tax levied every year is based on one and a half per cent of an assessed rental value so it is not usually excessive.

Tourism is the largest 'industry' on these islands, including the US Virgin Islands, with at least 60 per cent of the workforce engaged in some form of related work. Health facilities are especially good for such a small group of islands.

Cayman Islands

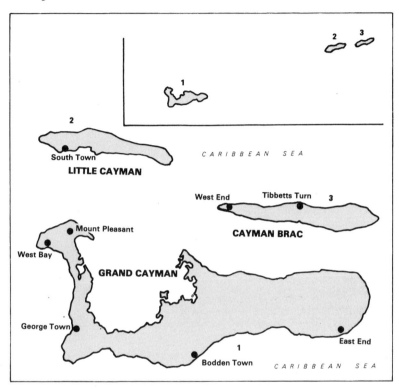

Status: British Dependent Territories
Currency: Cayman Islands dollar
Capital: George Town
Area: 259 sq km (100 sq miles)
Population: 16,677
Language: English
Longitude: 81°W   **Latitude**: 19°N
Average temperature: 27°C (81°F)
Annual average rainfall: 1570 mm (60 in)
International airport: Owen Roberts International Airport
Contact: Cayman Islands Government Office, 17b Curzon Street,
 London W1Y 7FE   (01 408 2482)

The three islands in this group cover some 100 sq miles of which Grand Cayman is by far the largest with a population of over 10,000. Cayman is a Carib Indian word meaning crocodile, and early explorers certainly found the reptiles waiting to greet them. Sadly they have gone, but a grand welcome awaits the visitor and investor. Fewer than 100 people live on Little Cayman, about 1800 on Cayman Brac.

The climate is hot on these flat islands, and the occasional hurricane and 'north-westers' do brush past. As with many islands the 1980 Hurricane Allen caused damage there, especially on Cayman Brac, but the last serious damage was in 1944. Most modern houses are built to withstand these occasional inconveniences.

If, like me, you are as captivated by the scenery below the water as you are by that on land, then these islands are well worth a visit as they have some of the best coral reefs to explore in the world. On land there are more than 50 species of bird to watch out for, plus butterflies and turtles.

The Cayman Islands have virtually no unemployment, but non-Caymanians must obtain work permits if they intend to work here.

Property is expensive. Although there are apartments for around US$100,000, or a little less, most immigrants look at the detached houses which cost from US$250,000. There are a number of estate agents on the island and a modern land registry exists. Stamp duty, paid by the purchaser, is seven and a half per cent of the purchase price, but in every other respect the taxation is negligible. Useful literature, including lists of estate agents and lawyers, can be obtained from the Cayman Islands Government Office.

The Channel Islands

The trouble with living on an island is that one's horizons become narrow. Despite the ease of access to both France and England, people who reside on one of the Channel Islands have to be positively prised off to go visiting. My taxi driver on a recent trip to Alderney, a man of about 35 summers, had never been off the island save for an occasional fishing expedition to Burhou, a tiny bird sanctuary teeming with puffins and rare flowers.

The Channel Islands have been loyal to England since 1066, but with a dialect of old Norman French still occasionally spoken and used in certain legal transactions. Land on the islands is measured in *vergees* which are about one fifth of an acre. The land area totals 75 sq miles and the population is approaching 130,000.

Jersey is the largest of these islands and covers 116 sq km (45 sq miles); its capital is St Helier and nearly 85,000 people live permanently on the island. The second largest island is Guernsey, approximately 65 sq km (25 sq miles) in area, with over 55,000 residents. In addition there is Alderney 8 sq km (3 sq miles),

Sark 5 sq km (2 sq miles), Little Sark, Herm, Jethou, Lihou and countless other smaller islands. Together they form part of the Armorican Massif of France.

The climate is mild with considerably more sun than mainland Britain. Frost and snow are rare and rainfall averages around 33 ins a year. With such a benign climate a prosperous horticultural industry has developed. The islands' loyalty to England, in addition to the comfortable climate and attractive tax concessions, have attracted many wealthy mainlanders. In addition, every year about half a million tourists visit the islands.

Jersey

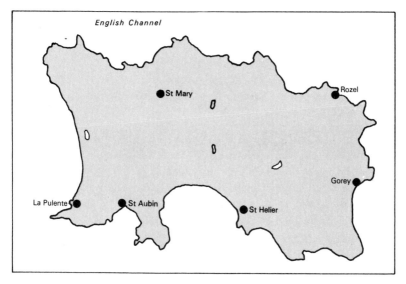

Status: The States of Jersey
Currency: Pounds sterling
Capital: St Helier
Area: 116 sq km (45 sq miles)
Population: 76,050 (1980)
Language: French/English
Longitude: 2° W   **Latitude**: 49° N
Average temperature: 20° C (68° F)
Annual average rainfall: 860 mm (34 in)
International airport: Jersey Airport
Contact: States of Jersey Tourism Committee, Tourist Information Office, Weighbridge, St Helier, Jersey (0534 31210)

Jersey, the largest of this group of islands, and one of the most popular tourist resorts, is nevertheless one of the hardest places in the world to move to. Small wonder, when the tax is only 20 pence in the pound on income. It has been described as 'the most exclusive club in the world' because fewer than 10 outsiders are allowed to buy houses there every year.

It is no good being merely a millionaire! To stand a chance of being accepted on this island one has to be a millionaire several times over, and of impeccable character. An alternative to amassing enormous wealth is to marry an islander. The only other option open is to employees and professionals whose skills are needed on the island. These could include doctors, dentists or the employees of major island companies, and even they are normally limited to a three-year stay. Applicants for residency are expected to have a taxable income 'comfortably in excess of £250,000 per annum'. This, in fact, means closer to £ half-a-million per year and the income must be derived from liquid assets probably valued above £6m. But pensions are taken into consideration. Applicants must first meet the Economic Adviser, who at present is Mr Colin Powell, and his recommendation to the Housing Committee is absolutely vital if the application is to succeed.

A few years ago one had only to be wealthy to move to Jersey but now the number of immigrants is strictly limited. Houses are classified into 11 different categories and only one, known as 1(1)K, is available for overseas purchasers. The maximum annual intake was recently reduced to five. To make matters worse, even this number is not exclusively limited to UK applicants - billionaires from all over the world seek the tax sanctuary of Jersey, with an additional bonus of its equable climate.

The realistic minimum price of a 1(1)K property is currently around £250,000, or a little less in the case of a flat. Normally there are many houses well in excess of this price. An added irritant is the limit on the amount of land an immigrant is allowed to retain for his own enjoyment (this is currently one *vergee*). Anyone buying a property with more than one *vergee* is obliged to rent the excess land to a local farmer. Consent from the island's Agricultural Committee can be sought for its retention, although this may not be forthcoming. Despite all these restrictions there is never a shortage of applicants for residency, indeed as many as 40 wealthy potential immigrants apply every year. In a nutshell, the wealthier the better, although islanders appear to have an aversion to the more brash, 'pop-star' type of wealth. The earlier in the year an application is made the better chance it has of receiving consent. Somebody with as little as £6m might stand a chance in January, whereas by Christmas time when most of the allocation has been made, considerably more assets would be needed. Ah well - perhaps next year!

Guernsey

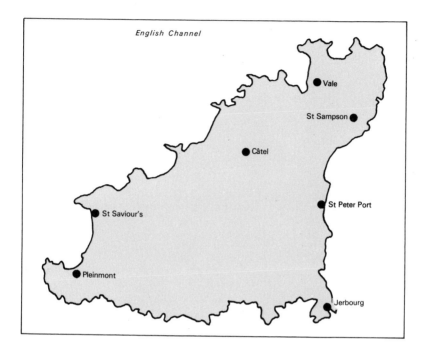

Status: The States of Guernsey
Currency: Pound sterling
Capital: St Peter Port
Area: 65 sq km (25.1 sq miles)
Population: 53,268 (1981)
Language: French/English
Longitude: 2°W **Latitude**: 49.5°N
Average temperature: 20°C (68°F)
Annual average rainfall: 848 mm (33.4 in)
International airport: Guernsey
Contact: Guernsey State Housing Authority, Albert Pier, St Peter Port, Guernsey (0481 24546)

There are really only three ways of setting up home on Guernsey, this little island in the Gulf of St Malo, 129 km (80 miles) south of the English coast, and all require something of a commitment. You can certainly move there if you are rich, it is after all a tax haven, alternatively you will be accepted, welcomed even, if you have some exceptional expertise which is lacking on the island; or you can marry an islander. The best way of obtaining an island home is to save up your pound notes and buy one of the 1600 properties on what the islanders call the 'open market'.

It is easier to set up home in Guernsey than it is in Jersey. The Open Market Register was started in 1957 and, with only one exception, no available properties to non-islanders have been added since that date. The purpose, of course, was to prevent wealthy outsiders buying up all the property and inflating prices beyond the grasp of local people. Effectively the cheapest house on the register is currently about £200,000. Curiously, some of the properties on the 'local market' (i.e. those available only to islanders) now change hands for considerably more than this. This is because the original register was assessed on rateable value, and farm houses which were not highly rated at the time have now been brought up to date. The islanders therefore enjoy a wide choice of houses and prices.

The rock bottom price for an 'open market' house would buy something like a Victorian town house with three bedrooms and a small garden. Detached houses are more expensive, costing between £250,000 and £400,000, whilst one with a piece of land could command £500,000 or more. The record price paid for a house on the island is now above £1,250,000. Cottages on large estates cannot be sold off on the open market since they have local market status.

Although Guernsey, in common with many other places, suffered some unimaginative developments just after the war, there remains a wealth of attractive houses. Some of them exhibit a curious stone projecting from the gable - this is the witch's stone, offered so that the harridan could park her broomstick there rather than on the chimney from which she might fall into the house. The island's purge of those unfortunates accused of witchcraft is a chapter of grotesque inhumanity which is hard to reconcile with the hospitality and charm of today's residents.

Despite the clement weather, the camellias, cheap wine and good English television reception, I suspect that the motives for most people moving to Guernsey are more mercenary. Income tax is low (20 pence in the pound) and residents are spared such things as VAT, capital gains tax and capital transfer tax. A further bonus, is that local household rates are low, averaging no more than £150 per annum. Conveyancing charges are reasonable, although a local solicitor must always be used. His fees, together with stamp duty, and a local feudal due called *congé*, work out at about five to to six per cent of the purchase price. After purchase, the new resident must register with the Housing Authority within 90 days of moving in.

It is essential, when contemplating a move here, to understand the laws of inheritance, as they are different from those of England. Whilst it is all right to bequeath cash, shares and objects to whoever you wish, the actual bricks and mortar must always pass to the deceased's immediate family.

Theoretically absentee property owners may not conduct a holiday letting business in their house, although long lets of 90 days or more are permitted. This does not mean, of course, that friends and relatives may not use the house for holidays. The only time-share development on the archipelago is La Grande Mare Country Club in Vazon Bay close to dramatic red granite cliffs. Currently prices for weeks range from £1600 to £14,000. Standards are high and resales have proved successful.

Alderney

The third largest island in this group and the closest to England is Alderney. It is a healthy, breezy place, populated by resilient and strong islanders, most of whom find no reason to leave even for a holiday. It is a botanist's and ornithologist's dream. When the Germans moved in during the Second World War, two colonies of gannets also invaded the rugged rocks off the island, Ortac and Garden Rocks. Unlike the Germans, however, the birds stayed and prospered. The little uninhabited neighbour, Burhou, is worth a visit. Lobster fishermen will give you a lift in exchange for a pint.

The island population of a little over 2000 elects its own Parliament which consists of 12 members, three of whom retire each year, plus a President who serves for three years. There is no tax other than a 20 per cent flat rate income tax.

71

This island has one big attraction which the others do not offer. There are currently no purchasing restrictions whatsoever on freehold property. The only restriction is that outsiders cannot build a new home on a building plot.

Although not cheap by comparison with the mainland, there is certainly more scope here for the less affluent than on the larger islands. My own choice would be one of the Georgian town houses with two bedrooms, which can still be found for around £80,000. Alternatively, modern bungalows tend to range in price from between £75,000 to £150,000. The normal rule of thumb is, the better the sea view, the higher the price. Prime agricultural land is generally under £2000 per acre.

Sark

They do not worry about petrol strikes on Sark because there are no cars. The few shops are mostly situated along a track known locally as The Avenue. There are perhaps a dozen hotels and a holiday on this tiny island is certainly recommended before considering any kind of house purchase there. Of 400 permanent residents, none pay any taxes. It is a feudal place, the current Seigneur is Michael Beaumont, the grandson of Dame Sybil.

The island is divided into 40 tenements (freehold farms) which cannot be further divided. These occasionally come on to the market. Each tenement owner sits on the island council knows as the Chief Pleas. Some tenements have only one house on them, whilst others might have as many as a dozen. A tenement, even a small one, would command a price in excess of £250,000. The only other way to purchase a property on Sark is to buy the lease of one of the surplus houses on a tenement. Currently a 40-year lease on a little cedar house with a large garden would command a price of about £70,000.

There is an excellent ferry service from Guernsey. The ground rents are low and life in general on Sark is really rather enviable. Again, the laws of inheritance should be noted; a man cannot disinherit his son.

Cyprus

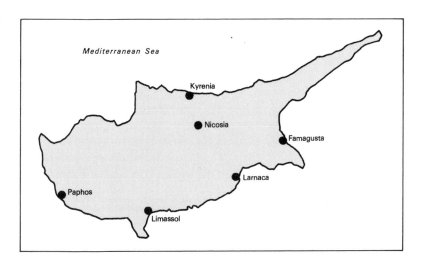

Status: Independent Republic
Currency: Cyprus pound
Capital: Nicosia
Area: 9251 sq km (3572 sq miles)
Population: 648,600 (mid-1983)
Language: Greek/Turkish/English
Longitude: 32°E **Latitude**: 34°N
Temperature: Varied: 29°C/9°C (84°F/48°F)
Annual average rainfall: 536 mm (20 in)
International airport(s): 2; Larnaca, Paphos
Contact: The Cyprus High Commission, 93 Park Street, London W1Y 4ET
(01 499 8272)

On a tree outside the underground church of Saint Solomini at Kato Paphos, in Cyprus, a thousand coloured handkerchiefs and ribbons flutter in the breeze from passing cars, pinned there by relatives of the sick in a simple belief that doing so will effect a cure. Faith like this plays an important part in the lives of the people who live on this island, and though they love the British, they remain perplexed and disappointed that we 'allowed' 37 per cent of the 9251 sq km (357 sq mile) island to be occupied by Turkey after the invasion of 1974. It is still a divided island, though there are no manifestations of the political impasse, other than the border controls in Nicosia. Not that conflict is anything new to Cyprus. As with many islands in the Mediterranean, particularly those in strategically important positions, people have been fighting for control of her charms for thousands of years. Before the division which amputated resorts like Famagusta, Greek and Turkish people lived, worked and worshipped side by side quite contentedly, even though the two cultures were quite different.

Although the island gained its independence back in 1960 the influence of the English lives on. On a recent visit to the island I was told by the Minister of Commerce that investment from the United Kingdom was high on the list of priorities; the islanders, he said, copied us in many respects. Legislation, property registration, and even driving laws were based on those of Great Britain; that is to say that they usually drive on the left, but not always - drivers being more rustic than reckless. A quarter of the Cypriot population currently lives in Britain. This 'marriage' of minds is not surprising when one considers that in addition to the many servicemen still in Cyprus there are nearly 3000 permanent British residents and several thousand more that own property there. Personal taxation is very low indeed, and the cost of living is among the cheapest in Europe. Before buying a home in Cyprus, an application must be made to the Council of Ministers on the island, and for permanent residency an application is made to the District Officer in the chosen area. Forms (M67 and Comm:145) are in English and may be obtained from the Consular Section of the Cyprus High Commission, or better still from the country itself through their Cyprus lawyers. In addition to the forms the office has some very helpful literature about day to day living on Aphrodite's isle.

There is a limit to the amount of land a foreigner can own on the island. Currently this is two *donums*, which is two-thirds of an acre. This means that one cannot go and buy one of the ancient vineyards, but your help at harvest time would always be welcome. For someone contemplating retirement to Cyprus there is a minimum income qualification. For a single person this is C£3000, while a married couple must prove an income of C£4500. There is an additional requirement for C£1000 for each dependent child. (C£1/£1.20).

Although many people do speak English a knowledge of Greek will be helpful. In the colourful markets measurements are by *okes* (one *oke* weighs just under three pounds). There are some strange words too which might prove confusing: *nay* means yes, a word sounding like 'okhee' means no, while 'thank you' sounds like 'Ef Harry's toe'!

There is now a great deal of new building, but mercifully a halt has been called to the high rise buildings of a few years ago - four storeys are now the absolute limit. Many Britons have enjoyed seeking out the near-derelict village houses; these usually have a pleasant secluded garden area and almost always sport one of the traditional Kleftico ovens, perfect for cooking lamb wrapped in carob leaves. On our way to one mountain village we passed a lemon grove with water being drawn by a blindfold donkey circling endlessly round an ancient alakati well. These village houses are always 'negotiable' when they are on the market, so it is not easy to get a precise valuation. Certainly there are some to be found well away from the coast for below C£8000, but full legal title deeds may not exist. While there has been a great deal of development around the more popular tourist honeypots such as Limassol, it is Paphos that attracts the British investor most. It is an area where a state of *ennui* would be impossible; there is even skiing on the high mountains. Here can be seen the pillar to which St Paul was tied before receiving 39 lashes for his preaching; here too can be found some of the most breathtaking mosaics in the world, most notable of all perhaps being the house of Theseus.

It can get very hot in Cyprus, but it is a dry heat to which one soon adapts. The west coast provides superb bathing, for cooling off during beach picnics. Even so a log fire is pleasant during winter evenings, but so far as energy costs are concerned, I found that most new buildings had solar panels which represent huge energy savings. One English family told me they switched on their immersion heater for only three to four weeks every year. The panels are not aesthetically pleasing, indeed some spoil the architectural line of the buildings, but the better homes have been built with features such as mock towers which disguise them. About 70 per cent of new homes have solar panels.

The Cypriot people are charming, and still much influenced by family bonds and the church. Honesty is almost assumed, few people trouble to lock cars or homes, there is very little crime. One youth who did break the law was so contrite that he eventually joined the police force!

Some of the laws relating to property are a little quaint, largely because it was inconceivable (I was assured) that a Cypriot agent or developer would break his word. Such assurances will not cut a lot of ice with sceptical English lawyers, however, and legal advice is as strongly recommended here as anywhere else in the world. Most Cyprus lawyers speak English, and there is a register of lawyers available: in the case of the west coast, from the Court of Paphos. When buying one of the older houses there is no problem about getting proper legal title, but things are a little more complicated in the case of new property. The Land Registry Office will not issue full title to property until the developer has completed all the roads, leisure facilities and other so-called 'infrastructure'. People buying in the early stages of development are therefore advised to lodge a copy of the contract at the Land Registry.

There is no capital gains tax on resales of a home, and provided money was imported through legitimate channels, there is no problem in taking out what you spent in the first place. However, profit from a sale can be taken out of Cyprus only in stages of C£5000 a year; thus if a profit of C£20,000 were made, it would take four years to get it all out. An alternative, of course, is to sell your Cyprus home to a fellow Briton. But he in turn could face the same delay in getting his profit out, plus the profit made by you, and so the cycle continues with most people selling outside Cyprus.

Inflation is not high but two years ago property values did start to rise, so the question of profit from sales became more significant. In the last year, values have increased only in line with local inflation, which is low. One can still buy a small studio-apartment around Paphos for as little as C£12,000. Some of the best are being built by Michael Leptos, who was one of the people forced to flee his home near Kyrenia during the Turkish invasion, leaving his house (now thought to be a restaurant) and several unfinished developments. Of course, when it comes to homes the sky is the limit. Several of the villas currently under construction are palatial with prices of C£700,000 by no means exceptional. VillaMed Properties represent several leading developers, and currently have villas at the village of Souni on the lower slopes of Troodos starting at C£40,000.

A flat in one of the exclusive holiday complexes would produce a good rental return, possibly above seven per cent a year on the investment. A one bedroom flat costs from around C£17,000, while one with two bedrooms will probably be approaching C£30,000. Larger three bedroom units are closer to C£40,000. For a more permanent home one might consider a villa in a development by an old vineyard above Paphos, where the cheapest house would be about C£30,000, but for that price you would be purchasing a two bedroom semi-detached unit.

Rates, such as those charged by local authorities in Britain, do not exist in Cyprus. Instead home owners pay individually for services such as refuse collection and septic tank emptying (outside Nicosia there is practically no mains drainage), and for the water supply. However outgoings are unlikely to exceed about £300 a year. Residents have to buy their water, but it costs only about £1 per ton.

France

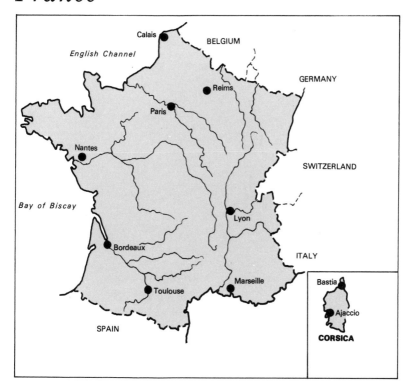

Status: Republic
Currency: French franc
Capital: Paris
Area: 541,110 sq km (212,730 sq miles)
Population: 53,963,000 (1981)
Language: French
Longitude: From 5°W to 5°E **Latitude**: 42.5°N
Average temperature: Varied 33°C/1.7°C (93°F/34°F)

Annual average rainfall: 700 mm (27 in)
International airport(s): 10; including two in Paris, others at Marseille, Nice and Lyon.
Contact: The French Embassy, 58 Knightsbridge, London SW1X 7JT
(01 235 8080)

Few neighbours could be so close and yet so different from each other as France and England. France is the country we hate to love, but do. She is the nation we least like to lose to at rugger, or soccer, and her inhabitants eat frogs' legs and cruelly-produced foie gras, and often drink their wines far too young. Judging by the noises produced by village bands they are tone deaf as well, but if France's songs leave a little to be desired, her wines and her countryside are beautiful enough to attract five million British tourists every year. And many of her visitors are sufficiently captivated by the buildings to buy a holiday or retirement home there.

France is more than twice the size of Great Britain (over 541,000 sq km (212,000 sq miles) in fact), but her population is a million fewer than ours. As any who have driven, hiked or cycled across her seemingly endless plains will testify, Western Europe's largest country has almost as many faces as she has wines.

The habits and preferences of French families, coupled with the country's laws of inheritance, mean that in addition to the many seaside areas meriting consideration there are also countless opportunities for investment in the vast and varied countryside ... from great crumbling châteaux to humble farm cottages and even barns. The successful Frenchman lives in town and sends his children to nearby state schools, but probably buys an easily maintained country home for weekends and holidays (the exact opposite, in fact, of his British 'cousin'). He would no more buy a derelict house, still less a barn, than put orange juice in his Bollinger.

The French do not recognise primogeniture and so every time the owner of a farm or estate dies, his land and savings are divided among the family. For this reason the once vast estates are now fragmented into countless small farms. Because of this fragmentation the French Land Commission (SAFER) has been trying to organise farming units of more practical size, and in extreme cases it might intervene in the case of a sale of prime agricultural property.

Generally speaking the French system of property transfer is fair and logical. Quite often it involves only the buyer, the seller and the public notary (*notaire*), who is impartial, although his fees are normally paid by the purchaser, as are those of the agent.

The *notaire* usually receives about two and a half per cent of the purchase price of the property, but on top of this the buyer has to pay taxes, including a Registration Tax which is similar to our stamp duty, although houses under five years old are exempt. Thus a buyer should allow at least 10 per cent of the purchase price to cover all his costs unless the property is new or nearly new. If the latter is the case then three per cent should cover these costs.

All property ownership is clearly registered at the Land Registry (*cadastre*), and only if the boundaries are being changed, or the property is being divided up, will it be necessary to engage a land surveyor (*géomètre*) to redraw the plans.

There is no such thing as 'subject to contract' in France. Once you have agreed to buy the property, and the vendor has agreed to sell it to you, both parties will sign a preliminary agreement, usually called the *compromis de vente*. The buyer will pay a 10 per cent deposit, either to the *notaire* or to the estate agent, but NEVER to the vendor, however honest his face. After the signing of the *compromis de vente*, both parties are legally bound to proceed, although there might be previously agreed 'let-out' clauses, usually if either party drops out from the agreement then they forfeit the deposit, or in the case of the vendor, an equivalent sum. Completion of the sale normally takes between 60 and 90 days but first the notaire will prepare the draft conveyance (the *acte*). This *acte* should be carefully examined by you AND your solicitor BEFORE the balance of the money is paid. Do insist upon receiving a copy of the draft as soon as possible.

If attendance at the *notaire's* office is difficult, it is possible to grant power of attorney for your solicitor (or someone else) to sign the documents on your behalf. Once signed, the *acte* is sent by the notaire to the Land Registry for official registration, though it can take a few weeks for the whole process to be completed. Avoid trusting the post for the transfer of important documents such as these.

Now a word of warning on buying new properties. Check to make absolutely sure that the property conforms with a proper planning consent and that there are no charges against it before parting with your money, even a deposit. In the case of new property, developers are required by law to be underwritten by a financial institution, so that if they collapse or flee the country, the customer is protected. Ask your developers if they have this cover. When the new property is within what the Americans call a 'condominium' then strict regulations apply to protect fellow owners' interests.

Probably the most convenient method of payment for your new home is by purchasing a bank draft or by direct bank transfer to the *notaire*. However, it is possible to open your own account in France and hold the necessary francs there which are needed to conduct and complete the business transaction.

Local rates (*impots locaux* or *taxes foncières*) are higher on land than they are on buildings. A château with about 16 hectares (40 acres), for instance, would probably cost the owner somewhere between 5000 and 10,000 French francs per year on rates. There was a wealth tax (*impôts sur la fortune*) on worldwide assets of above three and a half million francs until last year when it was repealed. This has brought a lot of French money back to France for many wealthy nationals are now buying property again. Do not forget that if you are planning to retire to France, you will naturally be subject to the taxation laws of that country and these are assessed quite differently from our own in the United Kingdom.

Recently property prices in France have been static, even falling in some areas, partly due to the uncertainty surrounding the country's left-wing government.

When the time comes for you to sell then the whole procedure is of course reversed. You, the vendor, should not be liable for any legal charges, even if the eventual buyer decides to engage his own *notaire*. In this instance, the two *notaires* share the fee. However, you will be subject to the laws governing the country and especially with regard to capital gains tax. This tax is applicable on any excessive profit made from the sale of your home, although allowances are given for inflation and so on; however, it is deducted immediately after the sale. As with most countries covered in this book, there will be no problems in repatriating your money provided that the proper procedures have been followed. Proof must exist as to where the money used for the purchase came from outside France.

Mobile Home

If all you seek is a holiday foothold in France, or perhaps a trial run without taking the entire family fortune out of Britain, one might do a lot worse than try a mobile home. True, they are towed to the site on which they stand, but once in position they are, in fact, anything but mobile. Despite this, Britons still remain prejudiced against these units. 'Not my cup of tea, actually,' is a common reaction from uninitiated Britons who envisage serried ranks of tired-looking caravans surrounded by washing lines, noisy children and run-down cars, with awful cooking smells and unspeakably close encounters with primitive sanitation. Nothing could be further from the truth at some of the sites I have visited, where the average profile of a holiday-maker is that of a successful businessman with a young family and a new BMW or Mercedes. Most looked astonished when asked whether they might not have been happier in a package-holiday hotel somewhere.

Hitherto the great risk for owners of mobile homes has been that of the owner of the site deciding to treble the rent or, worse still, finding some more profitable use for the land. The owner of the unit can then be faced with the nightmare of not only finding a new site but also moving his rather immobile 'mobile' home to it.

The industry in recent years has not enjoyed a good 'press'. Stories about rogue salesmen selling one unit to three or more individuals were not uncommon. Now, however, a more responsible attitude is prevailing thanks to the industry of firms like Haven Leisure, a subsidiary of Rank Organisation.

FRANCE PORTUGAL & SPAIN

FROM BRITAIN'S LEADING OVERSEAS LEISURE PROPERTY DEVELOPER

Mont d'Azur, Valbonne, Côte d'Azur – Country houses on a private estate with unrivalled views to the sea and the Alpes Maritimes. 2,900,000 FF.

The Old Village, Vilamoura, Algarve – A unique village in classical 18th century style architecture. Apartments and houses from £39,000 to £189,000.

Super Valmer, Nr St Tropez, Côte d'Azur – Provençal villas on a small estate with stunning views across the Bay of Cavalaire. 1,100,000 FF.

Montpelier I, Almerimar, Almeria, Spain – Freehold marina front apartments on this unspoilt South Eastern coast. £45,000 and £75,000.

Full management, rental and maid services. Leaseback discounts available.

For further details, simply telephone us now on 01-589 3400.

Montpelier International plc

17 Montpelier Street, London SW7 1HG

Haven Leisure has holiday parks all over Britain and France as well as a flotilla of 360 boats in France. In 1987 it arranged no fewer than 400,000 holidays. There are two sites in France: the first I visited was Les Charmettes, at Royan, which is on the Charente Maritime and is not far from the Côte Sauvage and near La Rochelle. The second site, Le Lac des Rêves (the Lake of Dreams), is close to Montpellier and right beside the Carmargue, that birdwatcher's paradise. Both were a short drive from magnificent beaches and close to shops and excellent restaurants. Facilities on the sites were designed to permit the enjoyment of a holiday by both parents and children. Ample supervision is provided for young children at swimming pools and games areas. But before buying one of these units, I recommend that first you have a holiday in one of them, just in case mobile homes are not right for you.

If you do decide to try out a mobile home, a car is essential, and most people take their own vehicles. The sites in Brittany are easily reached by the Brittany Ferries service, although the greater length of the voyage means that this costs more than most other alternatives.

If you decide to buy from Haven Leisure, then this involves the purchase of the mobile home itself and the assigning by the company of a 10-year lease for the site on which it stands. Thereafter, owners pay an annual rent and maintenance charge which is index-linked to the French cost of living. The units can be let, sold or bequeathed. In the case of letting, Haven Leisure does exercise some control over the type of tenants it permits. High spirits being what they are, four teenage boys, for instance, would not generally be regarded as perfect neighbours for a family with very young children. Income from letting should make a significant contribution to the family's holiday fund. Between May and September there is at least 75 per cent occupancy on the sites.

One of the problems with a mobile home, also common with some forms of time-sharing, is that one cannot expect the sort of capital appreciation which might be realised from the freehold of a villa or farmhouse. The life of a mobile home is finite, though to be fair, there is very little to go wrong with them. If a panel gets damaged it is easily replaced.

French regulations prohibit the use of mobile homes as principal residences, but this only means that they cannot be occupied for all 365 days of the year. In practice, the homes offered for sale by Haven Leisure are really not suitable for winter living, even though they do have built-in fireplaces.

Prices at the time of writing start at around £3500 for a good second-hand model which is around 8.5m (28 feet) long; the purchase would rise to £8000 for a brand new one. Annual charges are currently between £750 and £1100.

When the 10-year lease comes to an end, it does not necessarily mean that the mobile home must be removed. Provided it has been properly maintained and has not become an eyesore, the lease will be renewable on an annual basis. Each unit is connected to all the services, and stands on a plot of 150 sq metres

(1614 sq ft) or more. Some owners have created pleasant gardens around their holiday homes, though the annual charge does include basic gardening such as lawn mowing.

All in all, a mobile home in France, with the ability to exchange with owners on other sites, could provide family holidays of an acceptable standard, subsidised by the rental income, and could also form a base for someone seeking a more permanent abode.

Côte d'Azur

Try as they do, no region has managed to reproduce the ambience, or as the French call it 'snobbisme', that now oozes out of every corner of the South of France along the coast between Monte Carlo and Antibes. With the possible exception of Venice and a few more recent pretenders, the Côte d'Azur is where the rich prefer to be seen. Why this is so I cannot explain. The sea has many a hue, changing hour by hour, but then so it does in Cyprus. The weather is warm, but seldom as warm as in Marbella. The restaurants are tempting, but none so good as some in Beaune. There are casinos, pretty girls at every turn, hurly-burly, dress shops so expensive that most husbands prefer to avoid them, but above all an air of confidence - the sort of confidence an Olympic sprinter might be forgiven for displaying when lining up for the fathers' race at a school sports day.

This confidence also manifests itself in the sort of prices that would-be participants must now pay for a toe-hold on the Côte d'Azur, though there was a brief moment when France's politics recently caused the hearts of a few property speculators to flutter. It was perhaps a good thing that a brake was put on price increases because they were beginning to get out of hand.

It all started just over 150 years ago when our then Chancellor of the Exchequer was delayed on his journey to the Italian Riviera by a cholera epidemic. Lord Brougham was forced to stay in a tiny French fishing village called Cannes, and his statue still smiles benignly towards the old harbour. If those stone eyes could see I doubt whether the old Chancellor would smile, for modern Cannes is about as like his pretty village as the M1 is to the Romans' Watling Street. Now the beautiful people come for the film festival, as much to be seen as to see. They come to play the casino - a studio within staggering distance of the roulette wheel can cost as much as a château inland.

If I sound scornful it is because modern Cannes and Nice are about as French as Big Ben. The real France is to be found in the old town of Antibes, above and close to which are several developments where millionaire status is not a prerequisite. Indeed I recently saw some excellent studios in Val d'Azur for below £50,000.

There are still some unspoiled pieces of coastline, and a villa on the cliffs is perhaps the ultimate dream of most successful people. But dreams cost rather a lot. A villa which I viewed recently some 13 km (8 miles) from Cannes, on dramatic red rocks above that strangely blue sea was priced at £1,200,000 - exactly

the same as a stupendous old château a few miles inland in the quaint town of Bargemon. The château, surrounded by its own vines and olive groves, was in fact owned by an English family. The town is a delight, with fountains and streams feeding the pools where local women still do the early morning family laundry watched by a rather nosey journalist on his early morning jog.

There is still a lot of development going on in the South of France, some of it good and some ugly. I quite like the Port-la-Galère complex; it is a strange cluster of dwellings sculpted in concrete into the cliffs a few miles west of Cannes. It is the creation of the French architect Jacques Couelle. Each unit has its own private balcony.

But best by far, perhaps the most daringly brilliant holiday concept of our time, is Port Grimaud. It is set in the marshes by the sea below Old Grimaud, one of the loveliest old towns in France. At a time when most developers were building towards the sky, the architect, François Spoerry, was trying to persuade planners to allow him to create his childhood's dream - a lagoon town - a Venice without smells. They took some convincing, but within the town is a square name Place du 14 Juin 1966, the date when Spoerry finally received the go-ahead to start his monumental scheme.

We tried to count all the bridges, but failed: suffice it to say that there are many. The town, now nearing completion, is beginning to look as though it has been there for a couple of hundred years, or more. It is a short boat ride from Bardot's beloved St Tropez, another place, like Cannes, which was lovely without all the people.

There is a church in Port Grimaud as well as a bustling market where local wine can be bought from an English 'rose' who married the vigneron. Cars are banned from the streets, except for the delivery of luggage. Shopping and visits to the bars are usually done by boat. Most of the pastel-coloured Provençal houses have direct moorings on the 27 hectares (67 acres) of waterways, though a few studios and flats in the later stages do not. Letting potential here is exceptional - a house with moorings commanding £1500 a month, or more, during the high season.

If you like boats (lovely islands are but a morning's sail away), and you are reasonably gregarious, the Frenchman's Venice could be your answer. There is even a desert island for the children to sail to for picnics and adventures.

Country property

There are, of course, many alternatives to the Côte d'Azur for people seeking property close to the sea. For instance, there is the Languedoc-Roussillon area around Perpignan where many of the French take their holidays, or there is the much more beautiful La Rochelle, on the Atlantic coast. There are the vast and often rugged coastlines of Brittany and Normandy, including the so-called Emerald Coast, which have some of the best beaches and scenery in Europe,

and certainly more than their fair share of good sea-food restaurants.

However, not everyone wants the sea all the time. True, its colour and moods are constantly changing, but then so are the colours and seasons in the rural areas a little further inland, and here is where the real and unadulterated France is to be found. What could be better than the golden-yellow light of a warm autumn day in the Dordogne - the *vendage* almost complete, the walnuts falling, and the tobacco, so fragrant when drying, all combine to make this area one of the most civilised in the world. It is a tranquil scene, with pigs rooting around for those prized truffles; and I, for one, could live very nicely on walnuts and Pomerol.

The Dordogne River, and its lesser known tributary the Dronne, meander through some of the loveliest countryside, past quaint and unchanging villages. Amazing property bargains can still be found here, though the search is getting harder. Near derelict farmhouses, many with the distinctive *pigeonnier* tower at the side, are no longer so common, but neglected village houses still remain in plenty.

At the time of writing, Rutherford, in London, was selling several properties in the village of Montjoie, to the south east of the Dordogne. The village was built on a hilltop in the Middle Ages, and some of the houses have hardly been touched since. Many are jettied, with the first floor extending beyond the facade supported on massive timber beams, and although in a state of dilapidation these houses often contain superb architectural features. A little two-up/two-down was priced at just a few thousand pounds and had a valuable fireplace worthy of any home. Alas, there was no garden.

A more realistic price would be needed to buy a habitable home, in the region of £25,000 or so. Close to the sea, places like La Rochelle, in the Charente Maritime, village and country properties costing £10,000 or less can still be found. A typical village house in the pleasant village of Aulnay, with three rooms on each floor, costs around £11,000. One of these houses which I saw was in good structural condition, but required modernisation, and it also had a sunny courtyard garden. For the more adventurous there are barns and farmhouses. If you prefer life without such adventures the cost can be greater because you will then be competing against the French, most of whom would not countenance buying anything derelict. In recent years taxation has put second homes beyond the grasp of many French families.

Superb properties in France also exist a lot nearer to home, in the Deauville area, close to Le Havre and even closer to beautiful Honfleur. A number of London-based agents, including Farrar Stead and Glyn, have started selling country properties there, and the opportunities are most exciting. Normandy was always the region to get through as quickly as possible *en route* to the rich south, but for those with a mind to linger, and sample the cider and the architecture, Normandy with its mild climate has much to offer. The houses are among the prettiest I have seen. Most of them reveal heavy and complex timber framing with brick or plaster infill. The roofs often have highly decorated ridge patterns and pretty gables; roofing materials include thatch, tile and occasionally those beautiful oak shingles. Only one old craftsman still makes the slips of wood for this last method of roofing, but I am happy to report that he has a strong young apprentice. The shingles can last for centuries.

In Normandy many people have converted the old *pressoirs* (cider houses) into homes, and there are still a few awaiting this type of attention. Again, they are becoming scarcer. There are not many of the real bargain-basement properties such as those mentioned in Dordogne villages here, but £20,000 to £30,000 would secure a nice little *nid d'amour* in the country Of course, you can spend a lot more, and there are some excellent new developments close to the Deauville Golf Club with apartments starting at around £50,000. Properties in this area could prove a shrewd buy once the Channel tunnel is opened.

Châteaux

There are about 40,000 *grands châteaux* in France, many of them in a state of decay — rambling anachronisms in an age when the emphasis in building is on simplicity of style and economy of space. It takes a special kind of person to take on one of these great houses, either very rich, like Rolling Stone Mick Jagger, or the late Laura Ashley who also owned a property in Port Grimaud, or totally eccentric. The houses are impossible to heat, draughty, and a permanent drain on the money box. But they are also stunningly beautiful, and those enjoying a listing in the 'Caisse Nationale des Monuments Historiques' will qualify for substantial grants, both for repair and maintenance, especially when the owner is prepared to allow occasional public access. There are two categories of listing: Classified Monuments Historiques (equivalent to our Grade I), and Inscrit sur L'Inventaire Supplementaire des Monuments Historiques.

Contrary to popular belief, a château is rarely at the centre of a vineyard. Even the meaning of the word château is somewhat obscure. To the French it means simply a large country house, though *chasteau* (the circumflex replaces the 's') can mean a castle. The first châteaux were fortified homes, *Chateaux Forts*, but after the invention of gunpowder, which changed the established patterns of war, the new houses became known as *Châteaux de Plaisance*, opulent residences which retained only vestiges of military architecture. This change of emphasis coincided with a Renaissance of interest in fifteenth century Italy and classical forms of architecture. It took a century for this renaissance to drift across Europe, but the eventual fusion of the two styles manifested itself in these stupendous buildings, both sacred and secular. The climatic differences caused variations, of course, particularly in roof design.

Many of the châteaux are still owned by French families, a lot of them titled but hard-up. These homes have been in the same family for generations and there is seldom a rush to sell them, many remaining discreetly on the market for two

or three years, sometimes longer. One English family who bought a château in Burgundy now run a château agency. Patricia and Philip Hawkes own the Château de Missery and delight in telling visitors: 'Our Missery is our great joy'. It is truly a magnificent home: moated, with four circular towers, walled gardens, and lovely balustrades; its vastness could house an army with room to spare.

Years ago the châteaux of France would have been at the centre of vast estates, but inheritance laws, being what they are, have gradually broken up the estates. A few retain a couple of hundred acres, but they are very expensive. Generally speaking one gets a lot of château for one's money; indeed to build one today, if it were possible, would cost millions of pounds. The majority sell for below £250,000. One can still buy a château and a bit of land for as little as £50,000 (I once saw one described by Hamptons, as 'a challenge', but to get a habitable home a price of around £150,000 would be needed. For this sort of sum, one would become master of a property like the Château de Vaire le Grand, near Besançon, set in the beautiful valley of the River Doubs. It has five salons, a library and eight bedrooms (in need of restoration) plus a grand stone staircase, nine acres of formal parkland, and two large pavilions with about 20 bedrooms within. In addition, it has been included in the second category of listing which, with persuasion, could even entitle the new owner to financial help with the upkeep of the gardens.

Gibraltar

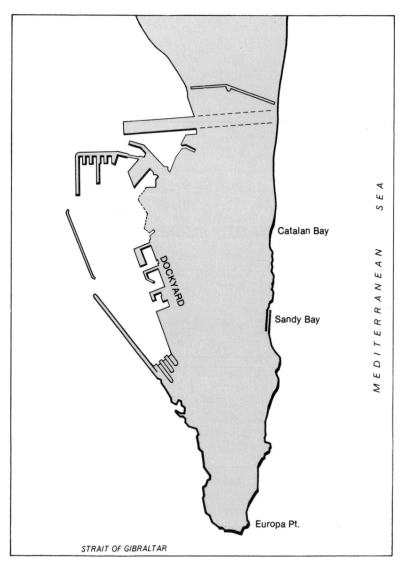

Status: British Crown Colony
Currency: Gibraltar pound
Capital: Gibraltar
Area: 5.5 sq km (2.12 sq miles)

Population: 28,719 (1981)
Language: English
Longitude: 5° W   **Latitude**: 36° N
Average temperature: 23° C (73° F)
Annual average rainfall: 605 mm (24in)
International airport: UK/Gibraltar flights from Gibraltar Airport
Contact: The Gibraltar Tourist Office, Arundel Great Court, 179 The Strand, London WC2R 1EH (01 836 0777)

It is said that so long as the tailless Barbary Apes (*Macaca Sylvana*) survive there, Gibraltar will remain British. Sir Winston Churchill himself even gave orders that their numbers should not be allowed to fall below 35. Had he lived long enough, he would doubtless have been delighted; recent breeding has been so successful that some are actually being exported.

This piece of rock, so strategically valuable throughout history with its labyrinth of 35 miles of underground roads, positively oozes history along its two and a half mile peninsular. The opening of the border, which became known locally as 'The Garlic Wall', marked the end of a 16-year blockade imposed when General Franco slammed shut the gates. The people of Gibraltar refuse to consider that Spain has any claim whatsoever to the Rock. When a referendum was held in this most English of places, only 44 voters out of the 12,000 wanted any links with Spain. However the siege left its scars on many of the lovely Regency buildings, with their Birmingham-made cast-iron balconies, many of which are in need of some loving attention. Even the once famous casino has become little more than an amusement arcade, but outside the entrance a framed artist's impression of the once proposed leisure complex is an epitaph to more prosperous times.

There are few freeholds in existence on Gibraltar, other than those granted in the last century. Ground-rents are high and even a modest leasehold flat can cost £80,000. Non-nationals enjoy considerable income tax advantages and there is no capital gains tax or property tax. The buyer pays all the costs of conveyancing, including solicitor's fees and stamp duty. With fewer than 2,000 bedrooms available in Gibraltar's remaining hotels, the letting potential of a flat is excellent. But owners must warn their tenants to turn off the taps firmly, for even the most prudent user can easily incur a metered water charge of £50 per month.

Gibraltar is London with sunshine, England without the rain. Policemen wear the London bobbies' uniform, Liptons tea and British bitter are available to wash down the dust and even the telephone boxes are postbox red! When it does rain, water is captured by a giant concrete slab on a cliff, but though adequate, 'Adam's Ale' is still almost as expensive as whisky.

The dispute over Gibraltar has simmered since the 1713 Treaty of Utrecht, which declared the island was British territory 'to be held and enjoyed with all

93

manner of rights for ever'. Gibraltar takes its name from Eby Tarik, a Moorish invader, the word *jibel* meaning mountain — Tarik's mountain. The 427m (1400 foot) mount has a remarkable diversity of wildlife and some fascinating museums and military establishments. Its climate is perhaps not quite as alluring as that of its neighbour's resorts due partly to the halo of cloud called the levanter which sometimes hangs like an ill-fitting toupée overhead for several days, putting people into a bad humour.

Building costs on Gibraltar are high when compared with Spain, but this is partly because British standards have to be observed and land prices are understandably higher. Gibraltar is a land of few houses and many apartments, but curiously it is getting larger as modern development, including new marinas, creep outwards into the sea. Paradoxically, the opening of the border has made access to several Spanish developments simpler and faster for British investors as they can now fly into its airport from London.

One of the most exciting developments currently underway is a £100m marina on reclaimed land at Rosia Bay, where Nelson's body was landed after the Battle of Trafalgar. The marina and properties are being built by the Wimpey Tricon Consortium.

Now that the Spanish government is on record as saying that it does not want Gibraltar against the wishes of the population, the future of this little bit of England seems secure.

Grenada

Status: Independent State/Parliamentary Democracy
Currency: East Caribbean dollar
Capital: St George's
Area: 344 sq km (133 square miles)
Population: 110,000
Language: English
Longitude: 12.06° N   **Latitude**: 61.43° W
Average temperature: 27° C (80° F)
Annual average rainfall: 1566 mm (61.66 in)
International airport: Point Salines
Contact: The Grenada High Commission, 1 Collingham Gardens, Earls Court, London SW5 (01 373 7808/9/0)

Grenada, often described as the most beautiful island in the Caribbean, forms a nation with its sister islands Carriacou and Petit Martinique. Mountains, rivers, lush rain forests and white sand beaches all contribute to the tropical atmosphere whilst the picturesque Carenage of St George's forms a charming focus of activity for the island.

The southernmost of the Windward Islands, Grenada is 19 km (12 miles) wide by 34 km (21 miles) long. Following a period of civil unrest which made the headlines of the world's newspapers in Autumn 1983, Grenada has enjoyed total economic and political stability. In order to buy land, application for a licence must be made to the Government under the Aliens Land Holding Ordinance. Foreign investment in tourism and property is actively encouraged, through tax relief and other incentives.

Ireland, Republic of

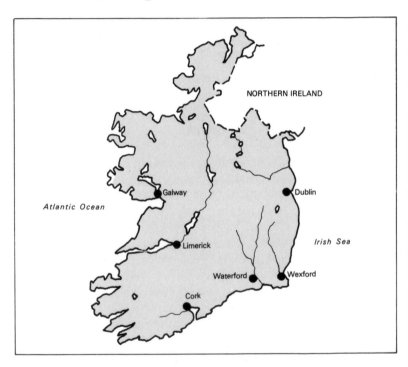

Status: Parliamentary Republic
Currency: Irish Punt
Capital: Dublin
Area: 70,282 sq km (27,136 sq miles)
Population: 3,480,000 (1982)
Language: English/Gaelic
Longitude: From 6°W   **Latitude:** 51°N

Average temperature: Varied: 20°C/1°C (68°F/34°F)
Annual average rainfall: 1106 mm (43in)
International airport(s): 3; Dublin, Cork, Shannon
Contact: The Embassy of the Republic of Ireland, 17 Grosvenor Place,
London SW1X 7HR (01 235 2171)

Snow sprinkled the top of the eight summits of McGillycuddy's Reeks the last
time I visited this beautiful corner of south-west Ireland, perpetuating the legend that the clan that has shaped the lives of the people there for centuries would
remain until the peaks went through an entire winter without the white topping.
The Gulf Stream warms this area but the mountains, close to Killarney, are the
country's highest, reaching 1040m, (3414 feet), and they have never failed to
show at least a smattering of snow on the top. The present McGillycuddy of the
Reeks is descended from Prince Oilill Olum, who died in AD234. Early Irish
genealogists described the Prince as the 43rd direct descendant of Mildh, who
trod the turf there around a thousand years earlier. The fact that the young
McGillycuddy has now sold the family estate without arresting the snow atop
the mountains has done nothing to diminish the legend, for has he not kept a
holiday home there for himself, to be sure. This land has stories and legends
beneath every pebble and a warm and welcoming people just bursting to recount them.

Though the Irish whiskey may not be quite so tempting as that of Islay, there is much to commend this area for both holidays and retirement. There are some remote and sturdy cottages on the west coast with the sort of views one would never want to leave; prices are the more attractive when one remembers that the Irish 'punt' buys only 80 English pennies. Not long ago I saw a cottage with two bedrooms on Coney Island by Rosses Point, in County Sligo, a place with its own pub and access by causeway for 16 hours of the day, and offered for only £IR22,000. There was also a three-bedroom cottage with views of the Atlantic from Mutton Island to the Cliffs of Mohar, with an acre of land, for £IR35,000; and another in Ashford, County Wicklow, with three bedrooms and an acre of garden, with views of the Carrick Mountains, for just of £IR40,000.

Buying property in Eire is no different from buying in England, and there are no exchange controls. While there are relatively cheap cottages and town houses to be found, estates and farmland can be more expensive than in many parts of England. Some 90 per cent of sporting estates are sold to non-Irish buyers. The market in Dublin, static for a few years, is now 'buoyant'. A large Victorian house in the Ballsbridge area close to the Royal Dublin Showground, can command £IR350,000 or even more.

The only important difference between our two countries came about a few years ago when the rating system was abolished. The new system (Residential Property Tax) relies considerably upon the honesty of the citizens who are invited to declare the value of their house and garden (agricultural land is exempt). Only property worth above £IR70,000 is assessed for tax, and then only if the combined income of the family is above £IR25,000. There was also tax relief for each child but this has now been abolished. Those that are liable to the tax pay one and a half per cent of the value above £IR65,000 each year. Stamp duty is severe. On property up to £IR50,000 it is charged at 4 per cent, on property between £IR50,000 and £IR60,000 it is 5 per cent while above £IR60,000 it is 6 per cent. Only new very small homes are exempt.

Isle of Man

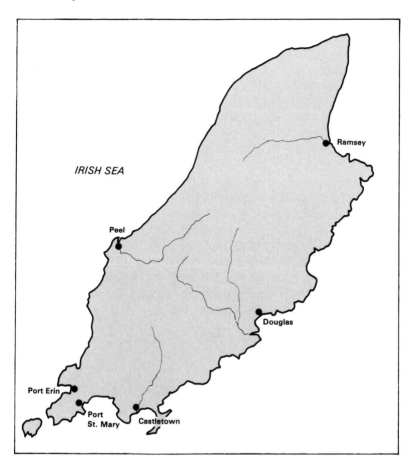

Status: Independent Sovereign State under the British Crown
Currency: Pound sterling
Capital: Douglas
Area: 572 sq km (221 sq miles)
Population: 64,679 (1981)
Language: English/Manx
Longitude: 4°W   **Latitude:** 54°N
Average temperature: Varied: 17°C/3°C (62°F/36°F)
Annual average rainfall: 1116 mm (40in)
Contact: Isle of Man Government, Government Office, Buck's Road, Douglas, Isle of Man (0624 26262)

It may look no more than a pimple on your school atlas, but the Isle of Man is in fact four times the size of the Channel Islands put together! The population on its 572 sq km (221 sq miles) is fewer than 65,000 (two-thirds of whom live in the capital, Douglas), under half that of those more southerly isles. The Isle of Man is a tax haven but unlike most others, it demands no financial qualifications for residency. It is an island of contrasts: even the weather can vary enormously. On the south side of the island, by the Calf of Man bird sanctuary, the weather is quite different from that of 31 miles away on the northern tip. Similarly, the scenery is extremely varied and the property available, both in style and value, also has many contrasts.

The English monarch is the Lord of Man, who appoints a Lieutenant-Governor. The island enjoys the oldest legislature in the world and celebrated its millenium in 1979. It remains fiercely, but not militantly, independent. Every year nearly 2000 people from the UK mainland, decide to move to the Isle of Man and make it their home: most are persuaded by its pleasant and mellow environment coupled with an appetising tax situation. Whether it is the weather tempered by the Gulf Stream, or the lack of personal taxation, or indeed a combination of the two, life expectancy appears to be remarkably high. There is a flat rate of 20 per cent for income tax, coupled with no stamp duty, property tax, or capital gains tax. The Isle of Man is even a cheap place to die, there being no capital transfer tax on the island.

The Isle of Man has its own National Health Service which caters for most day-to-day needs (chiropody is an exception) and private medical services such as BUPA are also available. In addition a reciprocal arrangement exists with the UK for the payment of pensions. It is altogether a most beautiful place for retirement for both the lazy and the active; golf is especially well catered for. There are some 500 miles of road on the island and running a motor car is cheaper than in Britain.

The ancient Manx language is seldom heard although a few residents still understand it. Religion and superstition walk hand-in-hand, even at the Annual Proclamation which is given in both English and Manx. During the two hour ceremony on 5 July, known as Tynwald Day, the clergy walk along a path strewn with rushes said to please the sea god, Mannanan, and even the bishop wears ragwort, the island's flower which locals call cushag. Ironically, it is against the local law to grow this yellow flower which is poisonous to horses.

Local customs are still respected, even by sensible 'comeovers'. Local elders would not dream of cutting down an elderberry for fear of displeasing the 'little people'. When crossing the Fairy Bridge at Ballaglonney, Douglas, it is wise to mutter 'Oie vie, vooinjer veggey', which loosely translated means 'good evening little people'. And never address the little people as 'fairies' for to do so is fatal !

Having its own legislature the island sends no-one to Parliament at Westminster. The Isle of Man government has its own upper and lower houses both of which meet monthly and which are known as the Tynwald. The island parliament consists of the House of Keys (taken from the Norse word *keise*, meaning chosen) and the Legislative Council. The former has 25 elected members who represent constituencies called *sheedings*. Meetings of the lower house are held regularly, commencing with prayers and then a school-like roll-call. Although it is independent from the activities of the mainland government, the Manx Parliament is of course influenced, but not necessarily persuaded, by Westminster. It did, for instance, agree to a system of VAT much like our own.

Sadly the ubiquitous spectre of unemployment has reached the Isle of Man, but things are looking brighter now, fewer than 1000 residents are without work. However, people wishing to move to the island may have difficulty obtaining a work permit unless their particular skills are lacking there.

During 1985 the Tynwald took a decision to encourage what they termed as 'economically active' people to the island. However, this only means that advertising will be directed towards the wealthy sector and there is certainly no intention of a discriminatory system such as that imposed in Jersey. The island parliament naturally wants to encourage the immigration of families who can support themselves and who are not likely to become a drain on the local economy.

As with the climate and scenery, the range of properties and architecture is considerable. In Douglas, for instance, which takes its name from two rivers, the Dou (black) and the Glas (clear), two extremes can be found. Perhaps the best bargains are located in the pretty garden squares surrounded by Georgian and Victorian terraces. This is where houses, some having six or even eight bedrooms making them ideal for conversion to flats for small guest houses, can still be found for around £40,000. To the front of these houses is the square and the central garden, while behind most of them, indeed behind many of the houses on the Isle of Man, is the all important *thie-veg* - the smallest room. Rooms in the house are usually lofty and some still retain attractive Victorian fireplaces, which in many other parts of the UK were replaced in the 1950s with the most prosaic models.

High above the town behind the new Summerlands (scene of a tragedy more than a decade ago), there is a modern estate of villa-style residences, with the name of Majestic View. Indeed, as the name suggests, the view of Douglas Bay is quite spectacular. Here the wealthy 'comeovers' sip their gin and tonics, not knowing that the mischievous locals refer to them as the 'when I' people — 'when I was in Kenya . . .' and so on. Properties up here are not cheap; indeed a figure above £150,000 would normally be needed to secure a home in Majestic View.

Building costs on the island are higher than those on the mainland UK and so some of the older properties are worth considering even if they do require modernisation. They, too, normally have the *thie-veg*, although now some do have the luxury of an indoor privy! A little cottage close to the 59.5km (37-mile) route of the annual motor cycle race might still be found for about £50,000.

Italy

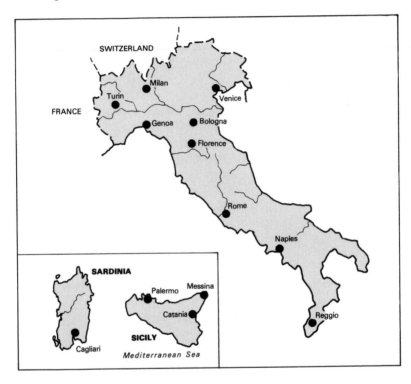

Status: Republic
Currency: Lira
Capital: Rome
Area: 301,247 sq km (116,303 sq miles)
Population: 56,223,000 (1981)
Language: Italian
Longitude: From 6°E   **Latitude:** 36°N
Average temperature: Varied 28°C/9.2°C (82°F/48°F)
Annual average rainfall: 675 mm (26in)
International airport(s): 25; including Rome, Milan, Florence and Venice
Contact: The Italian Embassy, 14 Three Kings Yard, Davies Street, London
W1Y 2EH (01 629 8200)

The shortest measurement of time has been described as that between the traffic lights turning to green and the Italian driver behind you putting his hand on the horn. However, if you can forget their road sense, or rather lack of it, they are a charming race, and their warm country has some of the most diverse and tempting property opportunities in Europe. Italians put great store on bricks and mortar, the ownership of which is of far greater importance to them than other tangible forms of wealth. Many outsiders are worried by the apparently volatile nature of Italian politics, but so strong is the Italian commitment to property ownership that fears of sequestration are unfounded. Such action, you will be assured, would require a genetical change in the inhabitants.

It is curious that Italy, more accessible than many parts of Spain, does not figure very prominently in overseas property advertisements and exhibitions. This is partly due to the fact that Italians tend to keep the best things, property and wine included, for themselves — and who can blame them for that. Naturally there is property for sale, but you will not find big sale boards or particulars with estate agents' panegyric to tempt you. Shoe leather will have to be worn out; but as many Britons have already discovered, the effort is well rewarded. Indeed, some that I spoke to beseeched me not to write about property opportunities in Italy for fear of attracting a lot of foreigners! So whilst I should not be telling you this, Italy does offer the complete escape. Unlike the more traditional markets of Spain, in some parts of which one hears more English spoken than Spanish, strangers are expected to at least make an attempt at the language.

We all know of the seaside resorts, the beautiful islands like Capri and Ischia and the enchanting towns and cities, such as Venice and Florence, all tempting in their own way; but for a permanent home go to the hills and river valleys of Tuscany and its southern neighbour, Umbria. There are mansions, cottages, town houses, derelict barns and even small vineyards available at sensible prices — although land itself is not so cheap. I recount the story of the German who thought he had been so clever making what he thought was a ridiculously low offer for a derelict farmhouse only to find it accepted. He had, in fact, paid double the going price.

It is difficult to write about Florence and its neighbours without it sounding like an eulogy, as the whole area was the tap root of the Renaissance; still further back in history it begat Etruscan and Roman culture. Every town is a history book of battles, sieges, religious milestones and fables. In Callodi, for instance, the story was written of an old man who dreamed of a wooden doll named Pinocchio turning into a real son. The area has a habit of making dreams come true. Not far from the hills of Tuscany is the coastline that inspired Shelley and Byron, while ski slopes are only a short drive away. Property gets more expensive as one gets closer to Florence, but away from the music and culture of that lovely city there is a lifestyle that appeals to people who like everything old, garnished with the delicious wines and foods (truffles and chanterelles for instance) that are abundant in the Tuscan countryside. The old houses have huge fireplaces, three-foot thick stone walls and rustic tiles. Many also include the beautifully formed archways typical of the region, and of course, there is some of the best marble in the world quarried nearby.

Although the land is not cheap, there is scope for an enterprising Briton with a knowledge of wine making to establish a vineyard, or to buy a going concern, and market his produce in Great Britain. The ownership of property in Italy is recorded with Roman precision, every house, shed and corner of land clearly marked and available for public inspection. Each town or local commune has its own register called a *Catasto*.

Having chosen your property your solicitor should check that there are no unpaid taxes from previous transactions for if there are you could become liable. He will, of course, also need to check that there are no sitting tenants or established rights of way that might have escaped your notice. Once this has been done and proved to be clear then it is normal to pay a 30 per cent deposit and sign a preliminary sale agreement called a *compromesso* or *promessa d'acquisto*. This deposit could be forfeited if you fail to proceed at this stage, while if the vendor drops out he will have to pay you the deposit plus an equivalent sum to compensate you for wasted time and expense.

The buyer pays notary fees and conveyancing taxes, which are calculated on the price shown on the deeds, called *rogito*. Traditionally this is between 50 and 60 per cent of the actual price being paid (i.e. the one shown on the *compromesso*). This is done with the apparent approval of the notary even though his fee will be calculated on the lower figure. Doing the transaction this way not only saves the buyer a lot of tax but also the vendor a lot of capital gains tax, INVIM (*Imposta Nazionale sul Valore degli Immobili*), but do take sound advice on this point. In years to come there is a chance that you could be liable for greater capital gains tax if the customs, rather than the rules, were to change. Not that the *invim* is terribly high. It ranges between 3 per cent and a maximum (seldom reached) of 30 per cent, on a sliding scale. A profit of 100 per cent on a property would leave the owner paying only 11 or 12 per cent capital gains tax after the sale. However, the conveyancing taxes are not so small, except on new property which incurs only 4 per cent when it is bought from the developer. Established houses incur a tax of 12 per cent of the price on the *rogito,* while land its taxed at closer to 20 per cent. When buying a home with a substantial amount of land (more than a normal garden) the *Imposta di Registro* will take into account the fact that there is a house and apportion the tax accordingly at its own discretion. All property, be it a house, farm or flat, is sold freehold.

All foreign buyers are immediately issued with a tax number (*codice fiscale*). There is a dual taxation arrangement with the United Kingdom and so any income from the property will be taxed only once. The letting potential of property in Italy is good. In the ancient hilltop town of Barga, for instance, an English resident organises a two-month opera season during which time many visitors need accommodation. A beautiful town house in the Piazza Angelio with a terrace and two bedrooms recently sold for about £50,000. There are also village houses and barns needing restoration which are often sold for below £10,000, but do check that consents have been given for the conversion work before signing the agreement.

Not far from the ancient Umbrian town of Città di Castello I saw a massive 20 room ruin, ideal for conversion into five or six units, standing in two acres of grounds in open countryside. The price was £60,000. Another, even more derelict house, with a two-acre vineyard, was priced at £30,000. In the town a third-floor attic with a large roof terrace overlooking quaint roofscape was being offered for £15,000. This area is only three hours drive from the French border, or there are regular Alitalia flights to Pisa. The journey by car is worth every moment of discomfort if only to sample the 'Pecorino', (sheep's cheese) the wines of Italy's own Monte Carlo, the wild boar and the peculiar but delicious fungi from the hills.

When buying property in Italy be sure to transfer money properly, either through a bank or in cash form (but not lire). Repatriation of funds is not a problem provided this is done. With Italy's membership of the Common Market there should be no problem about setting up home there and even working. In the case of remote country property it is wise to ask your solicitor to check with neighbouring farmers to see that they have no claim to the land, and also confirm the adequacy of a water supply and electricity.

Sardinia

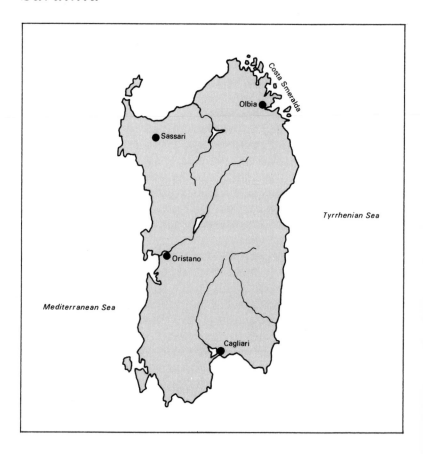

Well-meaning fathers bequeathed their best farm land to their favourite sons on this, the second largest island in the Mediterranean. The unproductive, rocky stuff next to the sea was normally left to the daughters; guess who has the biggest smiles on Sardinia. The coastline has some of the most beautiful scenery of any island.

This is a huge island; when I stayed in the exclusive Costa Smeralda, 3035 hectares (7,500 acres) paradise near the north, the capital, Cagliari, was 241km (150 miles) to the south. This is where the super-rich hide, and woe betide anyone who takes photographs in some of the more exclusive hotels where the residents and guests are definitely 'off-duty'. When I innocently snapped away beside a swimming pool an armed 'Caribinieri' was at my side in one bound; protests that I would actually rather be photographing the island's rare mufflons, griffon vultures or near-extinct seals (Foca Monaca) polished no buttons with my uniformed captor - but he eventually allowed me to leave.

A series of kidnappings a few years ago did Sardinia's reputation harm, but security is now very high and fortunately this crime seems to be a dying industry now. Costa Smeralda nestles beside a sapphire coloured sea (despite its name which means emerald) with rugged and uninhabited granite mountains to the rear. The development nearly didn't happen when, a quarter of a century ago, the young Aga Khan was persuaded to put some money into the venture. When he visited the site after a horrific sea journey and sleepless nights in a primitive hotel, the rain was lashing his face; the journey by jeep and on foot took hours...he was not amused. The only manifestations of human life were a few igloo-shaped shelters, built by shepherds.

Fortunately he did return, when the wild flowers were draped from the rugged cliffs, the sea had returned to its amazing colour and the sun was back in its proper place. The seed finally germinated and now 2,500 fabulous villas and apartments nestle among the natural outcrops of rock - some huge lumps, like sleeping mammoths, which dominate swimming pools and living rooms. Rustic tiles and huge irregular beams give these properties an air of instant antiquity.

The statistics are staggering. The development has 48km (30 miles) of coastline, and 32km (20 miles) of roads. The next 20 years will witness three more 'villages' with 5,000 units and two more 18-hole golf courses. The latter is intended to add to the beauty which Robert Trent Jones junior still believes to be his finest. It runs across a peninsular, and hackers like me would feel proud to so much as tread the turf. Other plans include two smaller nine-hole courses, sports complex and large tennis centre. Despite all this, the area is so large that only 5 per cent of the land will be affected, and strict rules apply here, as in the remainder of the island, preventing development within 146m (160 yds) of the beach. Those already built, owned by some of the world's wealthy are now almost beyond price. A computer, nicknamed Hector, can now calculate to the nearest pebble exactly what impact any building will have on a given area; previously the planners used sticks, stuck in the ground, the see whether roof heights and the like would spoil views.

Currently there is very little for sale below £100,000, save for a modest studio on one of the newer schemes; but there are some super building plots starting in price at about £60,000. Buyers should then allow about £100 a square foot for building, probably costing in the end about £250,000. Most people form an off-shore company when they buy. Any plans will have to be approved by the architectural committee which, until recently, continued to be chaired by the Aga Khan. There is no shortage of staff (everybody has staff, of course) and owners pay a total of about $1^1/_2$ per cent of the purchase price of their property every year for maintenance and management costs.

Seekers of local culture may be disappointed, however, as it can be found only after a drive away from Costa Smeralda. It is a little like a very up-market version of that television series called 'The Prisoner', except that no huge white ball chases those trying to leave; they are mostly content to stay, those who can afford the high prices that is.

Jamaica

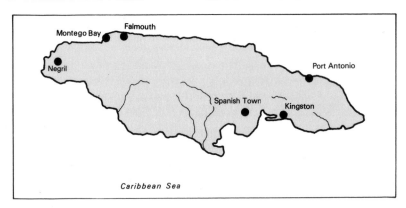

Status: Parliamentary Democracy
Currency: Jamaica dollar
Capital: Kingston
Area: 11,424 sq km (4411 sq miles)
Population: 2,200,000 (1981)
Language: English/patois
Longitude: 76° W **Latitude:** 10° N
Average temperature: Average 26° C (79° F)
Annual average rainfall: 1958mm (77in)
International airport(s): 2; Norman Manley International Airport/Donald Sangster International Airport
Contact: Jamaican High Commission, 50 St James's Street, London SW1A 1JS (01-499 8600)

We proceeded in a north westerly direction along Lime Street and into Cannon Street, past the ale house where Captain Morgan swore his terrible oaths; but the abandoned bottles contained only crabs and sea water, for we were three fathoms down at Port Royal in the entrance to Kingston Harbour, gateway to Jamaica - my choice as jewel of the Caribbean.

Lurking in those waters are the remains of the wickedest city in the west. At

11.40 in the morning on 7 June 1692, two-thirds of the town disappeared below the waves. Only a tenth of the 2,000 houses survived, and 2,000 people perished - a few more had miraculous escapes.

The remains are just one of many priceless archaeological treasures which Jamaica is hoping to develop in time for 1994, which will mark the 500th anniversary of the year that Queen Isabella gave this beautiful island to Columbus in recognition of his discoveries. His descendants still hold the deeds, but they won't do them much good now.

Jamaica is the third largest island in the Caribbean, covering 11,424 sq km (4,411 square miles) of tropical and mountainous terrain. Although a quarter of a century into independence, with only a Governor General appointed by the Queen to represent British interest, life there is still much influenced by events and traditions in the United Kingdom. They still drive on the left, for instance. Our love affair has lasted since 1655, when we grabbed it from Spain, and many Britons still own property there; I believe many more will join them when the island can get its message across the ocean that its residents are not all drug addicts and muggers.

Jamaica has not enjoyed the best of fortune in recent years. World demand for bauxite, which represented three-quarters of her visible export earnings, has plummeted; and exaggerated reports of her crime record and trade in ganja (marijuana) have dented her other great source of revenue - tourism. The only area in which I encountered reports of crime was in Kingston's Boy's Town, the home of West Indian cricket. Here rangy young blacks and grey-bearded sages plot England's downfall at Lords, practising with plywood bats and cardboard-box wickets. When I inadvertently jogged through the area the comments ranged from: 'Cool running man' to 'Hi, big man - you from the CIA?'

It was all harmless and good-humoured banter, but an understanding of the local patois, is certainly recommended. Everything has rhythm here: the language, the cricket, and even the reggae music, which I loathe in the English countryside seems just right here.

Jamaica has the oldest railway in the colonies, and if your get caught in the rain waiting for it just put rum on your head to stop the chill; they call it liquid sunshine there. When the train does arrive be prepared to have a goat or rooster for a neighbour - as well as laughter and chatter all the way.

To feel Jamaica, it is essential to get off the tourist routes. Walk, ride or drive through the jungles, past giant tree ferns, where at every corner you expect to see Tarzan swing by. With luck you will stumble on a village where they are cooking jerk port, soaked in allspice and ginger, and sizzled over pimento wood - quite the most delicious thing, but have a can of beer ready to cool the throat.

Most early mornings, I jogged through inland villages, watched by ubiquitous scavenger vultures called John Crows. The wildlife is abundant and so colourful it seems unreal. If you are very fortunate you might meet someone like

Lisa Salmon, the bird lady of Anchovy. Ms Salmon's house, near Reading, is feeding station to countless humming birds. The old lady - who resembles Gertrude Jekyll the great gardener, is myopic like her and also deaf - failing to hear the phone almost at her elbow. However, she recognised a nearby red-billed streamer tail by the sound of its feathers. There are at least 25 endemic species of birds; a glimpse of golden auriol or Jamaican mango hummingbird is enough reward for the journey alone.

That is Jamaica for you - a surprise at every turn, and most of them pleasant. Visitors must do the tourist trail, a feature like Dunn's River Falls simply has to be visited, even though it is a tourist honeypot, simply because it is so remarkable. Then there is the rafting experience on the Rio Grande. Apprentices have to drag the bamboo rafts a full 14km (8½ miles) through rapids, back to the starting point. They do this for at least two years before they are allowed to become 'Captains'.

Those apprentices will earn under £3 for their effort, but at nearby Trident Villas, one of the north coast's many superb hotels, a family of four would pay about £3,000 for a week's stay. Despite the obvious yawning gulf between locals and wealthy visitors, one seldom senses resentment. My raft 'Captain', Uriah Samuels, and his wife Ulith took me back to their bungalow in the village of Verrydale, near Fellowship, and feasted me on dasheen dumplings, yams, green bananas, mackerel rundung and bammie, washed down with soursop drink (fruit with nutmeg and rum) and another drink made from sorrel petals and ginger. Here was a hard-working and god-fearing family I shall never forget - added to which he has never turned over one of the rafts.

On Jamaica one never knows who one will meet next. The pleasant lady organising the boutique at Trident Villas told me her late husband was 'an actor'; he was named Errol Flynn. Up at Tryall Golf and Beach Club, 24 km (15 miles) west of Montego Bay, they host the most valuable golf tournament in the world. East of that bay is the Half Moon Club, which has some exceptional time-share houses and perhaps the best hotel in the world.

There are several very exclusive areas for housing on this island, but if one had to choose the best many would plump for those near Shaw Park Gardens, at Ocho Rios (eight rivers, though in fact there are more). Here a quarter of a million pounds would buy very little. The scope is limitless; there are very cheap houses, and up in the Blue Mountains, where the best coffee comes from, I met an English lady who was selling her colonial style house with 4 hectares (10 acres) for about £50,000.

Most estate agents on this island belong to the Jamaica Realtors' Association (PO Box 116, Kingston 6, Jamaica). Funds for the purchase of property must be imported through the Bank of Jamaica, and there are no mortgages for outsiders available. There is no capital gains tax, and foreigners selling their property are allowed to take out what they legally brought in. However, expect a delay in getting out any profit you might make from the sale.

Buying property is cheap and simple, but selling involves considerable expense. The vendor must budget to lose about 18 per cent of the sale price, as he is liable for the transfer tax ($7^{1}/_{2}$ per cent), half the Stamp Duty ($2^{1}/_{2}$ per cent), a small registration fee, the lawyer's fee (often 2 per cent, but some haggle down to 1), and the estate agent's commission, which is usually about 6 per cent. Buyers pay only half the stamp duty and legal fees, which together should be below 5 per cent. The local Bar Association will provide a list of solicitors. Good houses are available at all prices, from around £12,000 to £1 million. My choice would be a coffee plantation; the best beans grow above 1,000 feet, in the foothills of the mountains, some 500 plants to the acre. One needs a sloping site and about 2,000 plants to be commercial. Pat Wymore Flynn actually farms some 809 hectares (2,000 acres) on her ranch; there is something here for most tastes.

The Urban Development Corporation, formed in 1970, has done much to set Jamaica's economy back on the road. In my view, they made a mistake in building the magnificent conference centre at Kingston - the best beaches and golf are on the other side of the island, and that is what most people go to conferences for (if they are honest).

On a plaque outside the ambitious complex are inscribed the words 'One One coco Full Basket', followed by hundreds of names. Roughly translated from the patois it means that many beans are needed to fill a basket, and each contributes to the fullness thereof - the names are those of everyone, from humblest labourer to architect and directors who helped in the construction. The whole project, which cost £10 million, was completed in a year and is a tribute to the tenacity and ambition of a people whose motto is 'Out of many people, one people'.

Genetic remains of the original Arawak Indians, destroyed by the Spanish conquerors, can still be seen on the faces of some islanders. It is interesting to speculate what might have happened had the obscenity of slavery not existed; who would live here now? Many still resent the past, and some are now slaves to a new master, 'Ganja', but the 2,200,000 inhabitants live on the loveliest of islands. When they wave and say 'Hi bredder man - wa ah gwan man?' stop and buy them a beer 'hot or cold'. The smile probably disguises an empty purse. Considering the employment prospects prevailing at the moment, the crime rate is remarkably low.

Malta

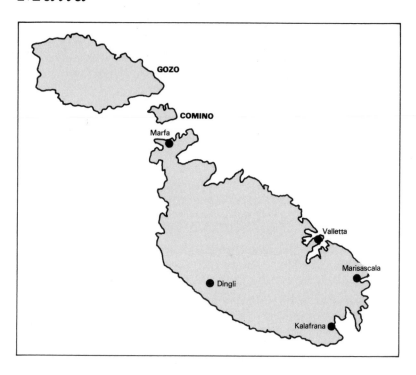

Status: Republic
Currency: Maltese pound
Capital: Valletta
Area: 316 sq km (122 sq miles)
Population: 364,000 (1981)
Language: Maltese/English
Longitude: From 14°E   **Latitude:** 35°N
Average temperature: 20°C (70°F)
Annual average rainfall: 578 mm (22 in)
International airport: Lugua
Contact: Malta High Commission, 16 Kensington Square, London W8
(01 938 1712)

If anywhere was deserving of a miracle or two it was Malta. It is a tiny island, less than half the size of the Isle of Wight, 93 km (58 miles) south of Sicily. Indeed, it is something of a miracle that there is still such a place. Malta, with its even smaller satellites, Gozo and Comino, was for centuries known as the nurse of the Mediterranean, but the nurse became a hornets' nest that frustrated our enemies and altered the course of the last world war.

For a whole month she endured the equivalent of the Coventry blitz every 18 hours. Small wonder the English monarch bestowed the honour of the George Cross upon the entire island in 1942. With the islanders on the point of starvation, a battered supply ship supported by warships to stop it sinking, limped into the harbour in the nick of time. Likewise, back in 1565, reinforcements arrived just in time to relieve the exhausted Knights of St John after heroic resistance against the Turkish hoards. The island's history is punctuated with tales of heroism and miracles. Many remember the massive German bomb that crashed through the domed roof of a church during worship to land, impotent, on the chancel steps. A replica is now used for collections.

Despite the savagery of the countless bombardments many of the island's houses and churches survived, as did the spirit of the people who lived and worshipped within them. A remarkable heritage of buildings remains, unbowed but scarred, housing one of the densest populations in Europe, nearly 3000 to the square mile. Among the 364,000 people living on the island are about 1000 Britons, while a further 3000 still own property there.

All has not been milk and honey in recent years; there have been many who regretted buying a holiday home there, but so dependent is the island upon tourism and like forms of investment for its survival, that a renaissance in brotherly love is promised. Dom Mintoff, ' the pocket Napoleon', was pledged to destroy all evidence of the century and a half of British rule - there even was talk of replacing the statue of Queen Victoria with a memorial to some rioters (or martyrs, depending upon whose side you take). But all true friendships have ups and downs, and now that Mintoff has relinquished the prime-ministerial reins things might get better; even most of the graffiti has disappeared. The Maltese people are engagingly innocent and hospitable almost to a fault, insisting that the two countries are as close now as they ever were.

Almost all of the Maltese speak English, and there are still plenty of fading pictures of the Queen on club walls. There are even red letter boxes, some of them Victorian. The fact remains, however, that it may take some time for the British to regain their confidence sufficiently to flock back to Malta as they did only a few years ago for holidays. British tourist figures slumped from half a million in 1980 to 270,000 in 1984. But there are signs of the numbers picking up.

A few of the British people who bought property there years ago have been frustrated in their efforts to sell it or, at best, been disappointed by the price it has realised. This has been largely due to the fact that the island is currently experiencing a 'buyer's market', - houses are cheap today; and so is the cost of living, for the past two years or so have seen zero inflation, with prices of some essentials actually falling.

As with several small islands around the world, a two-tier property system exists. Foreigners are allowed to buy a house or flat only if it is priced above £M8000 (about £14,000), and they can buy only one. Again, this is to prevent speculation in the property market, and so at least keep some homes within the grasp of the islanders themselves. If however you decide to buy a near ruin and spend a great deal of money bringing it up to scratch, you can sometimes buy property for below £M8000, so long as the total amount spent on the property, including the renovation costs, raises it above the threshold. Strictly speaking, foreigners may not buy houses of historic importance.

Once the decision to buy has been made, the usual procedure is for the buyer to pay a 10 per cent deposit. Normally this would be forfeited in the event of failure to proceed, so be absolutely certain you have chosen the right home.

If and when the time comes to sell, the owner is obliged to first offer the property on the local market where, strictly speaking, it should be sold only to a Maltese resident. In the event that there is no local buyer, the owner is usually allowed to advertise it elsewhere. There is no capital gains tax, and theoretically after the sale there should be no problem in repatriating the money provided it was brought in legally. A point to watch is the requirement of government approval of the value which the seller and his agent, between them, have agreed to put on the property. I have heard of cases where officialdom deemed the asking price to be excessive.

Very little new building is taking place at present for the housing market has been somewhat stagnant in recent years. Some of the apartment blocks, though in good locations, are looking a little tired by modern standards, but the good news is that prices are low. Best of all are the ancient farmhouses and village houses, approached down narrow lanes and looking rather ordinary from the outside. Ledges on the little windows (small to keep out the worst of the wind and the sun) often have a display of sweet basil, to signify the existence of an eligible daughter within; whilst over the doors bull horns are hung to frighten away evil spirits.

In between signing the preliminary contract and the final deed of sale, which would normally be no more than three months, the buyer should engage a notary public whose job is to establish the title to the property through searches. The notary will also submit the necessary applications to government departments. The costs incurred in the buying of property should not exceed about five per cent of the purchase price. This cost is made up of one per cent for the notary, 3.55 per cent for stamp duty, a Ministry of Finance fee of about £140, and finally something called a *Laudemium*, a once-only recognition fee paid to the original owner of the land. During negotiations it will be the notary's job to satisfy the Ministry of Finance that the price of the property is above the minimum and also that it is solely for use as a residence for the applicant and his family. In theory, the owner is not then allowed to let his property to other holidaymakers, but I gather that there is a diplomatic 'blind eye' turned when most people allow friends and relatives to use their home in Malta. The buyer will have to produce evidence for the notary that the funds used in the purchase originated from outside Malta, and the notary in turn, will have to satisfy the bureaucrats that this is the case.

People buying property in Malta may visit it as often as they like, provided their stay does not exceed three months. Longer stays can be arranged by an application for an extended tourist permit or one of two categories of permanent residence permit.

In 1988 new regulations aimed at encouraging foreign investment in Malta and her islands were announced by the government. They are complicated, but basically they are aimed at attracting wealthy outsiders seeking permanent residency. One of its main revisions concerns death duties; now tax will be charged only on the deceased's Malta estate, and no other assets will be taken into consideration. Also, income tax will in future be charged at a flat rate of 15 per cent on all income, less personal allowances. To qualify for permanent residency status an applicant must either have proven capital of about £258,000 (M£ 150,000) or an annual income of £17,200 (M£ 10,000), of which just over £10,000 must be brought into the island. A further £1,700 must be allowed for each dependant. The applicant must either own a house valued at not less than M£ 30,000 (or M£ 20,000 if it is a flat), or rent premises for not less than M£ 1,200 a year.

Unemployment there is high so a work permit is very difficult to acquire, writing is one of the few income-producing jobs permitted! Many Britons have chosen the island for retirement, although there are certain requirements that must be fulfilled before permission will be granted.

Older properties, with walls as stout as oak trees, have proved especially popular with British buyers. Though prosaic from without, they are usually delightfully cool and peaceful within, often having an inner courtyard, like a Roman atrium, with fountains and tropical plants. A few examples of current prices include an old village house in Zebbug in need of renovation, offered for M£15,000, and another nearby which has been lovingly restored, with large garden and swimming pool (for which an annual licence would have to be bought), costing M£15,000. Apartments in one of the better blocks were being sold for between M£18,500 and M£25,000 and these had annual maintenance charges of around M£500, which is high by Maltese standards, but the gardens and pool are excellent. New villas on the exclusive Santa Maria Estate at Mellieha, on the northern side of the island, cost between M£20,000 and M£75,000. The best property I saw, however, was owned by a British couple, and was built within the actual ramparts of the ancient town of Modica, whose architecture alone demands a full day's exploration.

There are many estate agents on Malta, offering houses on both the main island and on the surprisingly green Gozo nearby – 67 sq km (26 sq miles) as compared with Malta's 246 sq km (95 sq miles). There are still plenty of old homes awaiting restoration on this smaller island, the home for 10 years of Ulysses, according to Homer's *Odyssey*. Gozo is popular with the Maltese who if they can afford it, often own a summer home here. Tiny Comino, with its clusters of homes and a good hotel, is but 2.5 sq km (one sq mile) in area.

A group of about 20 of the agents has formed the Association, of Estate Agents, with an office at 7 The Whispers, Ross Street, Paceville, Malta. Together with the fine old Phoenicia Hotel, in Floriana, close to the capital of Valletta, they can organise special four-day property hunting packages, currently costing from £240, or £320 for seven days, with a promise of plenty of property to view and a car to explore the island included in the price. The journey is by British Airways, which offers an excellent service. However I found several Britons there who had motored down through Italy and then come over on the ferry, making quite an adventure of the journey.

One can live cheaply on these Maltese islands and find plenty to occupy the days. The wine is better than expected, as fragrant as the scented flowers and herbs found on the rugged hills. And the people? Friendly they certainly are, even if their driving does leave a little to be desired; they normally drive on the left, but not always. When the authorities put traffic lights on the island no one could remember which colour meant start and which one meant stop, so the posts now stand at junctions with no lights; it is safer that way.

Monaco

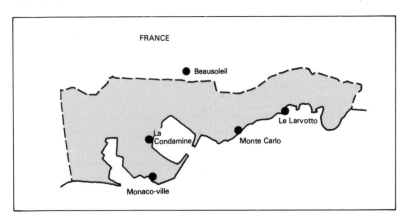

Status: Principality
Currency: French franc
Capital: Monaco-Ville
Area: 1.9 sq km (0.7 sq miles)

Population: 27,063 (1982)
Language: French/Monégasque
Longitude: 7° E **Latitude:** 43° N
Average temperature: Varied: 25.5° C/8° C (78° F/46° F)
Annual average rainfall: 786 mm (30 in)
International airport: *via* Nice
Contact: The Consul-General for Monaco, 4 Audley Square, London W1
(01 629 0734)

Seekers of tranquillity, butterflies and birdsong, blended with economy, will not need to put this tiny country, between Nice and the Italian border, on their short-list. Blades of grass are quite a rarity, but there is plenty of razzle-dazzle, roulette and racing cars. Even a walk on the beach at the country club can cost several thousand francs a year, but the key that members receive is said to 'open the gate to half the world's money'.

The last time I visited this tiny principality which is only slightly larger than the City of London (i.e. the square mile), The Monaco Grand Prix was weaving its ear-splitting way round the winding roads. The best view was not where I started, right beside the track, but high above the town, close to the royal palace, with the famous casino and harbour a visual reminder of the mind-boggling affluence of certain sections of the community. Many of the visitors that day were as much people-watching as they were racing enthusiasts.

Monaco, like Gibraltar, is nibbling into the sea and indeed there are some exciting new developments with first-class sports facilities springing up in this area. It is so small that one development is in Monaco but its tennis courts are 'abroad', in France. The border is real enough, but holidaymakers come and go without even knowing they are crossing it.

The resident population of Monaco is fewer than 30,000, of which only about 4000 are Monégasque - holders of the coveted Monaco passport. The remainder are French and Italian with a smattering of the wealthy from other countries, even Great Britain. Foreign residents, except those from France, enjoy considerable tax advantages, but the government is anxious not to encourage the building of tiny boxes which people can use simply as an address. To qualify for the tax advantages, people must either own a home outright or rent one with a tenancy agreement of at least one year. It is practically impossible for a foreigner to obtain Monaco citizenship, however.

One and two bedroom flats can be found ranging in price between 2,000,000 French francs and 5,000,000 French francs. The country has its own car number plates, coins and postage stamps.

On my last visit I watched tennis professionals battling it out for a few million francs on the hallowed courts below my apartment, before lunching at Le Roquebrune, at Cap-Martin. I then watched the Grand Prix before joining and

mingling with the 'beautiful people' at the Cannes Film Festival ... all very arti-
ficial, but quite appealing in small doses! But near me was a man who had
bought three large apartments for more than 12,000,000 francs and turned them
into one. Little flats were also available, for below 1,000,000 francs, but these
were intended for the maid. Club membership is also rather high - one does
really need quite a heap of money in the bank before trying to break the bank
or even live in Monte Carlo.

Montserrat

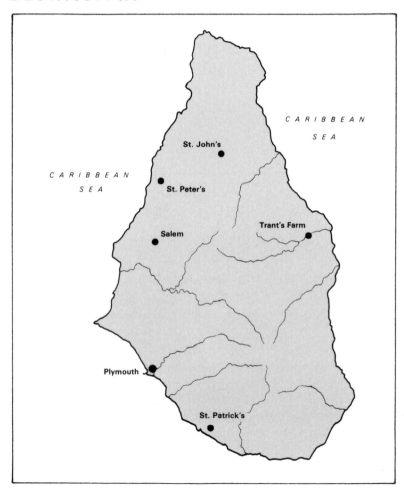

Status: British Dependent Territory
Currency: East Caribbean dollar
Capital: Plymouth
Area: 102 sq km (39 sq miles)
Population: 12,074 (1980)
Language: English
Longitude: 62°W   **Latitude:** 16°N
Average temperature: 26°C (79°F)
Annual average rainfall: 1525 mm (50 in)
Contact: Foreign and Commonwealth Office, Whitehall, London (01 233 3000)

Less than 30 miles south-west of Antigua, this island is one of the Leeward group and covers just under 40 sq miles. It is mountainous with its highest peak reaching over 3000 feet. The hills are covered with dense foliage and this coupled with pretty bays and blue sea further enhances the scenery.

Montserrat has several active volcanos plus one called Soufrière which sends out sulphur fumes. There are also some well-known hot springs on the island. It was Columbus who named the island, saying it reminded him of the Abbey of Montserrat near Barcelona.

Stamp duty is charged on the purchase of property and is based on a sliding scale, but there is no capital gains tax when selling. There is an annual property tax, and this again is on a sliding scale with a maximum of 20 per cent of any estimate rental value being charged.

Orkney and Shetland

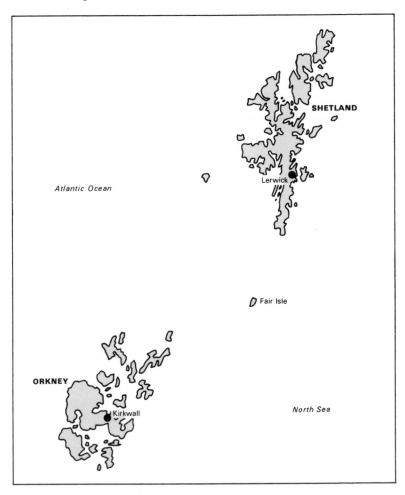

There are parts of the British Isles which are so remote, and so completely different from the mainland, that the sense of travelling and exploration is greater than that felt when visiting most other European countries. Of all the Western Isles, a stay in Jura can be heaven, not least for the comforting malts from neighbouring Islay, so peaty they taste like iodine. Then there is Lewes, wild and sometimes inhospitable, where the forces of nature put their shoulder behind the mighty Atlantic and squeeze the murky water into swirling currents between the islets, which are as close to Iceland as they are to London.

Further north still are the archipelagos of Orkney and Shetland (never call them the Orkneys or the Shetlands). Here is the tiara of Britain, blessed with the life-enhancing Gulf Stream that sometimes washes coconuts from the West Indies on to the sandy beaches. Here, in June, the dawn chorus seems to last for 23 hours; on an early morning stroll shadows cast by the sun make giants of children. The welcoming fragrance of peat fires always greets the visitor.

Unlike their neighbours on Shetland, who are fishermen who also do a bit of crofting, Orcadians are essentially crofters who do a bit of fishing. Fewer than 20,000 live on the Orkney Isles, nearly half of them in the towns of Kirkwall and Stromness and the remainder scattered across more than a score of the 67 islands.

Orkney has a healthy, if slightly esoteric, tourist industry with enough wild-life to satisfy any budding nature student. Its residents have, however, expressed concern at plans to build the world's largest fast-breeder reactor across the water at Dounreay, on the mainland). Many want to restore historic links with Denmark and Norway. The scheme brought a frown to the face of the Old Man of Hoy.

These islands stretch 80 km (50 miles) from north to south, and a welcome awaits even the Sassenachs, some of whom have set up home there.

A welcome also awaits the visitor to Shetland (or Zetland, as it should be called). The 100 islands, 1424 sq km (550 sq miles) of blest rock, are on the same latitude as Greenland, but thanks to the warming Gulf Stream its strong people enjoy a far more benign climate.

While it is of course possible to fly to Shetland, the best mode of transport, if you can pick a calm night, is on one of the two P&O motor vessels that are the chief life-line to these islands 996 km (600 miles) north of London. The 294 km (183 mile) voyage from Aberdeen takes about 14 hours, and 'soothmoothers' and 'incomers', as the Shelties call their visitors, are assured of a welcome.

At first glance these islands, treeless save for a few brave but stunted birch and lichen-covered sycamore, are not very different from Orkney, though the two are separated by treacherous sea streams. However, crofts on the northern group are very much smaller than those on Orkney, some having just a handful of acres. Also, an absence of voles on Shetland means the southern islands have a greater number of birds of prey.

The Shetland islands themselves are contrasting, as indeed are the people who live on them. Take Fair Isle, for instance, famous for its knitting patterns, where the God-fearing teetotal residents speak a dialect that puzzles even other Shelties. On Foula (derived from 'Fugl Oy' meaning bird island) they do like a dram. On this edge of the world several young families have recently joined the older residents - life is hard but rewarding.

Huge cliffs and peaks dominate Foula, where countless sea birds cling to the cliffs. Only St Kilda is higher than the 365 m (1,200 foot) cliff called The Kame. The birds have to learn to live together, as do the few humans that scratch a living there, growing crops in 'planti crubs' - circular stone walls that shelter young brassicas.

Although surrounded by oil fields, a phenomenon which caused an untypical boom and slump in Shetland house prices, petrol is as precious as water in the desert to the people of Foula, whose visitors are met at the landing strip by a tractor and timbrel.

Peat is the main source of warmth here, each croft owner being entitled to cut the equivalent volume of his home for his year's supply. Newcomers will have to master the art of cutting turf with a 'tushker' - no easy matter. When concern was expressed last year that the peat might run out an expert from Glasgow visited the island and calculated that enough remained to keep the inhabitants warm for another 1,250 years. The senior resident, of four score summers or more, commented after the public meeting: 'Aye, that's all very weell - but what do we do after that?'.

The older residents seldom leave their island; one woman born there 78 years ago left the island only once, when she broke her leg. She still walks six miles a day to stack her supply of peat. Her older friend, who survived the Burma road atrocities, has strength which is legendary even by Sheltie standards; he can still lift a 45 gallon drum from boat to shore.

So many young people are now carving out a life here that there is talk of spending £180,000 on a new school. Most residents believe the money would be better spent on a new harbour - they will build the school themselves.

Many of the islands which once supported scores, or even hundreds, of crofters are now uninhabited. However, the depopulation of Shetland was arrested after the war and in recent years there has been a steady increase of residents.

Despite the influx of new blood there appears to have been no dilution of Norse custom and dialect and several books have been published on the languages alone. The islands were handed to Scotland back in 1469 as part of the dowry for the Danish bride of James III. A puffin, for instance, is a 'tammy norie'; 'piri' means small, while 'muckle' means large.

When people on these smaller islands refer to 'the mainland' they are talking not about Scotland, but about the largest island in the group. Mainland is some 378 sq miles in area, with Lerwick its bustling capital.

A landmark in Scotland's history and also that of the islands was the controversial Crofters Holdings (Scotland) Act of 1886; it was necessary at the time but leaves the lairds of today with little income and still less influence.

It is possible to obtain a crofting tenancy, or even ownership, but the Crofters Commission keeps a strict control on newcomers. Only those of 'crofting status' are considered, which effectively means one has to be hard up and have previous crofting experience. Sometimes properties are 'de-crofted', giving outsiders a way in.

Others inherit a foothold, as did the laird owning the Isle of Vaila– 324 hectares (800 acres) which a century ago sheltered 100 souls. He has been trying to find a buyer for the island and its 300-year old mansion ('Haa') for some time. It is quite a kingdom, its western side with cliffs and 'Gaada Stacks' (huge holes in the rocks) being among the most spectacular sights in Britain. There the puffins were so stuffed with sand eels that they could only scamper along the surface of the sea.

Across the water, on the mainland, sits my favourite hotel in Scotland, perhaps the world. Burrastow House, its windows looking across to islets populated by otters, is small, but its food is amazing. An early-morning walk from there is accompanied by no sound, save for a busy oystercatcher and the occasional 'drumming' of a snipe.

Property laws are little different from those of Scotland, where gazumping is unknown. A few ancient customs, such as 'Udal Law' based on Norse word of mouth, might affect ownership of such things as the area of beach between low and high tide; apart from that there is nothing to worry about. Most estate agents there are also solicitors. A few ruins can still be found for below £10,000, but restoration costs are not cheap.

Once there, the resident can spend a lifetime exploring all the other islands: wild uninhabited places such as Noss, where Great Skuas (Bonksies) swoop and bang you on the head, and Eider Duck coo like grandma opening Christmas presents. Wild flowers, like spring squill and orchids, provide an early summer carpet. In 1876 a pair of those remarkable Fulmars nested on Foula, spitting foul-smelling liquid at intruders; now their numbers are almost too many to count, and they seem to live for ever. I can't promise newcomers eternal life, and I recommend several visits both in and out of season before buying a home there, but if any place in the world offers long life this has to be high in the league. If you join this exclusive community be careful what you say though - news travels faster on the island grapevine than it does on the phone.

Portugal

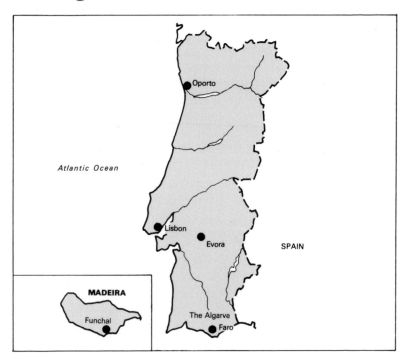

Status: Republic
Currency: Escudo
Capital: Lisbon
Area: 91,971 sq km (35,510 sq miles)
Population: 9,826,000 (1981)
Language: Portuguese
Longitude: From 6°W **Latitude:** 37°N
Average temperature: 17°C (62°F)
International airport(s): 5; Lisbon, Oporto, Faro, Madeira, the Azores
Contact: The Portuguese Embassy, 11 Belgrave Square, London SW1X 8PP
(01 493 3873)

Many Britons are beginning to look west of Cadiz for their holiday and retirement investment but Portugal's Algarve coast has so far been spared the mass developments seen in Spain. The country has perhaps learned a few lessons from the mistakes made along the still beautiful but much-scarred Costa del Sol. There are, of course, other areas of Portugal well worth considering. Developments like the Quinta da Marinha 809 hectares (2000 acres) of forest, golf courses, and beaches on the Estoril coast about 25 km (16 miles) from Lisbon is one. Then again, there are vast areas of rural Portugal stretching up to the port-producing regions where country homes of great charm can be found.

It is the Algarve, though, which has really caught the imagination of British investors during the past few years, and interest is growing all the time. It has a bracing and beautiful south-facing coast, washed by the Atlantic and protected from northern weather patterns by the Monchique and Caldeiro Mountains. Its name probably derives from the arabic *el gharb*, meaning west of the land beyond. Despite its rapidly growing popularity there are still many who are not quite sure where it is; one agent told me he often gets letters addressed to him at 'The Algarve, near Spain'!

The best way to explore the land is on horseback, along the gravel lanes that bisect the little farms. In the early morning I watched a smallholder and his son stoking charcoal clamps, while not 100 yards away a wealthy German family was preparing for bed after a late-late barbecue. Rustics and millionaires work and play side by side while both enjoy one of the lowest costs of living in Europe.

Early in the eighth century Moorish invaders swept through the Algarve and their domination was complete until 1189, when combined Portuguese, German and British forces took the Moorish capital of Chelb, known today by its modern name of Silves. Thereafter the rulers called themselves King of Portugal and the Algarves, emphasising the separateness of the regions. Today the main town on the Algarve is Faro, a name with Moorish influence said to mean the smell of dogs. It has an international airport that copes with an increasing amount of tourist traffic every year. It was from the Algarve, and from Sagres in particular, that Prince Henry the Navigator despatched his sea captains on the epic voyages of discovery. The school of navigation was established there because by the fifteenth century the River Arade alongside the once prosperous port of Silves, well inland, had become unnavigable.

The coast becomes more beautiful the further west one heads, on towards Sagres and Cape St Vincent, the very toe-nail of Europe. Round the corner and a short way up the west coast can be found miles of deserted beaches, with bee-eaters, crested larks and kingfishers as common as crows on the flower-covered hinterland. Here we ate, like four kings, with lashings of local wine for £3 a head! Food is never far from one's thoughts in the Algarve. The wines are excellent and varied, the bread is a wholesome meal in itself, and the chicken piripiri is memorable. Always meals are finished with a dangerous aguardente de medronho, distilled from mountain berries.

Despite a devastating earthquake in the region about 200 years ago, much of the building retains a moorish influence; but the most easily recognisable features of the attractive houses are the magnificent chimneys, often built free-hand by the bricklayers, with hardly two the same. The area is still considered to be an earthquake zone, but modern building regulations take account of this, largely eliminating the risks. More recently it was the political instability that dampened foreigners' enthusiasm for investment there, but those that stood firm after the bloodless revolution of a few years ago have seen their homes rise enormously in value.

After the revolution, development stood still for a while, but now it is all systems go, with championship golf course and villa 'cities' of the highest quality springing up along the coast. Tempting though these luxurious new buildings are, buyers should realise that there is a fairly hefty property transfer tax (called *the Sisa*), which can add at least 10 per cent to the purchase price. Currently the tax is charged at the rate of 10 per cent on all property except for first-time purchasers of homes at new developments costing less than 10 million escudos. This tax is charged only on the initial purchase. Thus if you buy only a building plot, or a derelict farmhouse, there is no further tax to be paid on the building work. The only trouble is that the tax militates against resales, for when the time comes to sell your home the people house-hunting in the area will also be hoping to buy just the building plot.

Take your time with the search for the right property. Things tend to move pretty slowly on this coast. There is a seven year wait for telephone installation, for instance. Once you have found your property both parties will be expected to sign a promissory contract (*Contrato de Promessa de Compra E Venda*), which is legally binding on both the buyer and the seller.

A deposit of at least 10 per cent is usually paid by both parties and this deposit is forfeited by either party in the event of cancellation before the signing of the *escritura*, the final exchange of title to the property. Usually the initial contract will include a copy of the licence from the Bank of Portugal for the importation of funds for the purchase, the licence is called, '*Boletim de Authorizacao de Importacao de Capitals Privados*'. The buyer signs the *escritura* in front of the State Notary, but if he cannot be present he may choose a representative, after which he will receive an official copy of the registration document; the original remains with the notary to be retained in the Land Registry, or *Conservatoria*. Legal and notary fees for these transactions average around four per cent. It is important to be legally represented during property transactions, if only because several members of the family selling the property may have different notions as to its value. It is a good idea also to draw up a new will as soon as possible, for laws of inheritance in Portugal differ a great deal from our own. A spouse does not inherit in the event of intestacy, the estate instead passing to the next generation.

Good references, proof of solvency and an unblemished character record are normally all that is required when applying for a resident's permit (*residencia*).

Particular care has to be taken when buying one of the many lovely old country properties. Some will have the original well (*nora*), with its long line of

buckets, but certainly it must have a proper water tank, a *cisterna*. The quality of life in the country is measured by the gallons in the *cisterna* - provided it still holds water, the local fire brigade will fill it for you during a drought for about £10. Having found your ideal old property do not engage the first builder who offers his services. There are hundreds of retired British couples in the Algarve - ask for their advice (or warnings), and insist on seeing some of the work your chosen builder has done. Standards range from abominable to quite good. A few people have tried to establish small agricultural enterprises of their own, but a run of years of drought has demoralised most of them.

It was perhaps inevitable that so innocent and beautiful a place as the Algarve should eventually succumb to the overtures of speculators, and so the area now has its fair share of bulldozers and ready-mixed concrete. However a rule has been introduced prohibiting any development within about 200 yards of the low tide mark, so consents that existed before this rule was brought in will mean that there will be a few very valuable properties in the coming years.

There are some superb estates within a short drive of Faro, including the 405 hectares (1000 acre) Vale do Lobo (Valley of the Wolf) development, with its golf courses and internationally famous tennis centre, currently run by our own Roger Taylor. The golf course on top of the red cliffs is challenging: one hole includes a drive across a ravine. Closer to Faro is Villamoura, a giant holiday complex, much of which I would not think suitable for permanent occupation, but admirable for family holidays. The Romans evidently liked this area for there are some splendid antiquities currently being excavated close to the marina.

Between the two is the Quinta do Lago (Farm of the Lake) which is perhaps destined to become one of the finest holiday and golf centres in Europe. It covers 1011 hectares (2500 acres) of pine-covered land by the sea, ablaze with wild flowers for much of the year. Several major companies are currently building holiday homes. There are also building plots for sale, but buyers are obliged to build on them within two years of purchase. A second golf course, designed by Floridian Joseph Lee, is under construction, and when completed it will have more than 40 hectares (100 acres) of fresh and sea water lakes in the landscaping. These lakes are being stocked with fish to keep down the mosquito population. Fish play an important, almost symbiotic part in Algarve life. They are a staple diet, and one of its kind, a fish called a *gambusia* is put into the *cisterna* of country properties to help keep the water clear.

Further along the coast there is the famous Penina Hotel and golf course, with a few exclusive villas and some time-sharing. Indeed you will find time-share properties in most major resorts here. Just up the road there is my favourite development called the Carvoeiro Clube, named after a little fishing village, as well as Monte Carvoeiro and Clube Atlantico which is nearing completion. Clube Atlantico, on cliffs above a former smugglers' cove, reached by some very expensive steps, will appeal to the more wealthy reader. Prices start at above

£150,000 for a three bedroom villa, but it will have a large swimming pool, marble floors, and a unique chimney stack, hand crafted. The Carvoeiro Clube has a tennis centre, and David Lloyd is one of the coaches; among its many other facilities is an excellent riding school. A new 27-hole golf course designed by Trent Jones is underway. The whole project was started about 15 years ago by a German family named Möeller, who came on holiday from Hamburg and decided to stay. The 61 hectares (150-acre) development is now completely sold out, but further land is being built upon providing more villas and an aparthotel. This establishment has a good letting potential. The Monte Carvoeiro development, set around a pretty square with shops, fountains, a jazz cellar (inaudible from above) and a fine wine cellar, is also completed. The bustling square is paved with a sort of coarse mosaic called *calçadas* very popular in the Algarve. This will be the focal point of all three developments, and among its shops, bars and other small commercial ventures there also will be an optician and doctor's surgery. Prices here are rather high. Even the little flats in the aparthotel, which measure about 55 sq m (600 sq feet) will cost about £40,000. Villas are priced between £150,000 and £250,000, but they are on a grand scale. A two bedroom and two bathroom town house in Monte Carvoeiro costs about £90,000.

The further west one goes along this coast the more reasonable the prices become. On the rocky coast road which leads from Lagos to Luz, we stopped at Burgau, where an English family runs a popular sports centre; we then went to Salema, past vast empty beaches of stunning beauty. The developer here, an enthusiastic Englishman, believes most families now strive for two holidays a year, and his villas and apartments are therefore geared for economy but with no sacrifice of comfort. A two bedroom villa with lovely views and a swimming pool can be bought for about £54,000 whilst one with three bedrooms and a pool costs £63,000 (pools add about £8000 to the cost, and away from the sea become almost an essential). Flats in a new beachside development range in price between £23,000 and £48,000. Time-share weeks in a Salema complex range from as little as £540 up to £3600.

Few people tire of Portugal, but in the unlikely event of an enforced move back to England there is currently no capital gains tax on any profit made.

AN ENGLISHMAN'S CASTLE

in Portugal

BUYING A HOME ABROAD

Buying a property overseas can be a rewarding experience. The formalities however, can become tedious and take the edge off the excitement. The Bachmann Group can take care of these problems for you and explain the benefits of Company Ownership and, with the support of legal and technical advisors, achieve a secure ownership structure.

Together with a major U.K. Clearing Bank, we can offer loan facilities of up to 70% secured on the shares of the property owning company. Loans are available for up to 20 years in any major currency at 2% over base rate in the case of sterling, and 2% over 3 month LIBOR for other currencies. The loans are available to finance stage payments.

THE BACHMANN GROUP

OVERSEAS PROPERTY SERVICES

Bachmann & Co Limited
P.O. Box 175, Frances House
Sir William Place, St. Peter Port
Guernsey, Channel Islands
Telephone   0481 23573
Facsimile   0481 711353
Telex   4191637 BACFID F

*BANKING · INTERNATIONAL TAX ADVICE · YACHT REGISTRATION
COMPANY AND TRUST MANAGEMENT*

Madeira

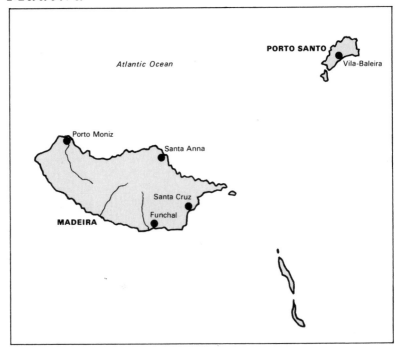

Nothing like Portugal, nothing like Spain, not even like the nearby Canary Islands, save perhaps Gomera, this sudden lump of rock smothered with flowers has long been a favourite of discriminating Britons. A brief stop at Funchal on a cruise is all that many see of it, but to say you know Madeira after that would be saying you know England after a day in Barking. Although Funchal, meaning the fragrance of fennel, is well worth exploring.

There are about a million Madeiran people in the world but only about 300,000 of them live on this archipelago; apart from the sweet wines with which old gentlemen sought to educate young maidens one of Madeira's chief exports is manpower. She also exports a wide variety of fruit together with wickerwork and exquisite embroidery, the last being a cottage industry employing about 6,000 women who earn 680 escudos (under £3) for every thousand stitches they do.

Many Britons have found a tranquil retirement here, though good property is not easy to find. There is always a good size congregation at Funchal's English church. As with most countries, the country houses are beautiful, but establishing proper title to them is not always easy.

Madeira, and its little neighbours Porto Santo (where Columbus found his wife Felipa) and the Desertas, hosts 48 endemic species of plants and countless other botanical treasures from all over the world; they prosper in a benign climate which can sometimes unleash a bountiful rainfall.

Most history books record the discovery of the archipelago by Zarco, representing Henry the Navigator, in 1418; he actually took sanctuary from storm at Porto Santo (hence its name) and spotted the larger island a year later. However, Britons pride themselves in the story that the islands were actually discovered by an Englishman who was shipwrecked there with his lover, Ana de Arfet, back in 1346. The village of Machico, where Zarco landed, was probably named after him.

What a dramatic prospect these islands must have offered those early travellers. The steep volcanic mountains and river valleys clothed in dense forest were an ineluctable invitation to explore. The name actually means woodland. Now visitors are greeted by quaint fishing villages nestling beneath some of the world's highest cliffs.

The best way to house hunt is to explore the 805 km (500 miles) of irrigation channels called 'levadas', which link the wetter north with the south. Like the roads they are planted with hydrangeas, agapanthus and other flowers; arum lilies grow everywhere there. Stopping in the village bars one might be successful simply asking: 'Is anything here for sale?'. Most will probably want to hire a car to explore, for nowhere is more than a day's drive from the capital. On the north side of this 58 x 22 km (36 x 14 mile) floating garden, waterfalls cascade on to the road giving everyone a free car wash.

By contrast there is tiny Porto Santo (Holy Port) which unlike its big sister has superb beaches - if you have the stomach for the ferry crossing. It has a few small hotels plus some of the best fish bars in the world; try the ugly but delicious 'espada', which lurk 3,000 feet below the surface of the sea.

Older houses are hard to find on both islands; those that survive have embellishments on each corner of the roof, and contain some of the distinctive blackish 'basalto' stone. Buying procedures can be assumed to be the same as those in Portugal, though things do proceed at an unhurried pace. One rule is strictly observed - shutters may be any colour so long as it is green!

There are some excellent hotels in Madeira, but air fares are not cheap. House-hunters may care to stay at the Savoy, or the famous Reid's; but for a more typical flavour try the Quinta da Penha Franca, or up in the hills, the Pousada Vinhaticos.

Little country ruins may still be found for below £10,000, if you are in no hurry; subsequent renovation costs would not be subject to the Sisa tax. Madeirans like large kitchens, a feature that will appeal to many British buyers. In Funchal itself the hills are steep, as anyone who has dared a ride on the wicker toboggans (called carro) will testify; perhaps older people will prefer to look for a home in villages elsewhere on the island. There are large apartments starting in price at about £40,000, while £150,000 would buy a magnificent clifftop home.

A few holidays here are definitely to be recommended before moving in permanently; it would be all too easy to fall in love with the flowers, the people, the honey cake and the beef cooked on a spit ('espetada'), not to mention the Madeira m'dear, and forget about the rush and hurly-burly awaiting you at home. Be sure you are ready for paradise.

Scandinavia

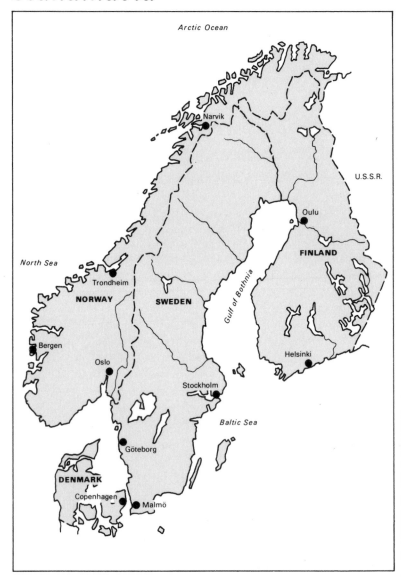

People in these vast countries tend to own second homes, and in most cases there is no problem about aliens getting a foot in the door. The standards of building leave us in the shade, but I doubt if the weather patterns will greatly appeal to Britons other than for holidays.

Some may find the lack of pubs in Finland a trifle tiresome; all business seems to be done in the saunas. Europe's fifth largest country, which begat Sibelius and countless javelin throwers, is a land of endless lakes and forest (65 per cent of the land is covered with pine and birch). Restaurants are of course allowed to serve alcohol, to wash down the roast bear, reindeer, fish and beluga; and there are plenty of candidates for Alcoholics Anonymous, who sometimes voyage on the ferry boats to commune with strong liquor. Everything is rather expensive, so take your own whisky.

Property conveyancing is simpler than it is here, all land being properly registered and available for inspection. A stamp duty of between four and six per cent is charged, depending on the price of the property; change of ownership must be registered within eight months or a penalty is incurred. A Finnish speaking solicitor is vital as forms of application to the country's government must be completed in the native language. A capital gains tax is charged on profit from resales, but after five years ownership this is usually waived.

Sweden too has some superb holiday home opportunities, both in the mountains and by the bracing sea. They are great outdoor people, and rejoice in 'Allemansraett' - everyman's right to go everywhere. However, they always observe and honour the country code.

A stamp duty of about $1^1/_2$ per cent is charged, as is a tax of the same amount on the land. There is also an annual tax, equivalent to our rates, based on the market value of the house.

How to buy a home in the sun without landing in a bunker.

Buy Bovis abroad.

<u>Bovis abroad</u> is good news for anyone who wants to buy a second home in the sun – with our name and reputation behind it, the purchase is safe, sound and worry free.

But for golfers, Bovis beats everything. Hole out in the Lakeside Village at Quinta do Lago (just one of three <u>Bovis abroad</u> developments in the Algarve) and you have – in one stroke – the golfer's paradise:

You're surrounded by 54 of the finest golf holes in the world. And with them, a whole range of luxury freehold properties from one bedroom studio apartments to detached villas with private pools.

If you prefer the fame of Spain, try this. La Manga Club. Frequently home of the Spanish Open. With Seve Ballesteros for the touring professional. And more prime villas and apartments.

LA MANGA Club

For full details, call 01-225 2215. Or write to: <u>Bovis abroad</u>, Dept. OP, 62 Brompton Road, London SW3 1BW.

(Call into our offices opposite Harrods and you can see our developments on video.)

Bovis abroad

P&O Group

We build in one thing extra. Peace of mind.

Spain

Status: The Spanish State, Kingdom
Currency: Peseta
Capital: Madrid
Area: 510,000 sq km (197,000 sq miles)
Population: 37,973,000 (1981)
Language: Spanish/Catalan/Basque
Longitude: From 3°E   **Latitude:** 36°N
Average temperature: Varied: 28°C/8°C (82°F/47°F)
Annual average rainfall: 419 mm (16.8 in)
International airport(s): 27 international airports including Madrid - Barajas, and those on the Canary and Balearic Islands
Contact: The Spanish Embassy, 20 Draycott Place, London SW3 (01 582 5921) (Mon-Fri between 9.30 am and 2.30 pm)

It has been said that Spain will be all right when it is finished, but there are parts of it which were better by far before they were started. A drive from Malaga airport along the main road, affectionately known as 'Death Alley', still passes many half-finished tower-blocks and hotels that were started a few years ago by undercapitalised builders. They are gradually being either completed or demolished but large sections of this once-idyllic coastline are ringing to the sound of bulldozers and concrete mixers. 'The world is moving south, and many of them want to come here' exclaimed one Marbella developer when I asked whether there might not be too much building.

But who can really blame the world, and who can blame the Spaniards for capitalising on that most enviable of natural assets, sunshine? The historian who wrote that God granted Spain everything except good government was not far from the truth, but this young democracy does at last seem to be moving into the twentieth century. The price of this movement is Spain's loss of innocence. The traditionally honest country has recently suffered what is known as a bad press following a rash of crime against tourists, a few of them of a violent nature. Now even one crime is one too many, but when one considers that more than half a million British tourists pass through Malaga airport alone each year, the record is not as bad as the newspaper reports might lead us to believe. It is not so much that Spain is a vipers' nest of crime, rather that it has, unfortunately, acquired the warts that afflict most civilised countries these days. Drugs are usually at the root of the problem, so cash is what is wanted. Spanish police have moved with uncharacteristic haste to manifest their concern; but wherever you have wealth you have rogues, so be on the alert and remember to lock up when you go out.

In the few years that I have been watching the property market in Spain I have witnessed a remarkable improvement in building standards. Cavity walls were almost unheard of a few years ago! The war against crime is a relatively new phenomenon, but developers have been quick to capitalise on its requirements, and most new developments now put great emphasis upon security. One also hears of fewer cases where people have been swindled, but as with crime, it takes only one or two adverse reports on shoddy buildings to sully the image of the whole country.

It also does not help the image of Spain to have British criminals 'cocking a snook' at the law from the sanctuary of their villas in Marbella. Fortunately, a new extradition agreement has been ratified between our two countries. Although not retrospective you should not have a fugitive bank robber for a neighbour when you move to your new home.

Spain, like most of Europe, does have an unemployment problem, and in their quest for work many young people are deserting the land and hill villages for the noise and clamour of towns like Torremolinos and Benidorm where the package-holiday family has to be fed, pampered, watered and entertained. This leaves a wealth of property away from the coast available at bargain-basement prices. Not that I have anything against Torremolinos. It was a pretty little place

Take your place in the sun

Moneysaver value to Spain

Low cost, seat only flights with departures every day. Flexible durations including weekends. Fully guaranteed. And only £25 for children under two to any destination.

Easy to book, instant flight availability. Booking and ticket issue at your travel agent with the new Iberia Saver System.

Iberia serves Alicante, Barcelona, Bilbao, Las Palmas, Madrid, Malaga, Palma, Santiago, Seville, Tenerife and Valencia.

For full details and reservations see your travel agent, or call Iberia.

London: (01) 437 5622, Birmingham: (021) 643 1953, Manchester: (061) 436 6444, Glasgow: (041) 248 6581.

IBERIA
AIRLINES OF SPAIN

once upon a time, but now it is a very large, crowded place which gives thousands of people a much-needed holiday of fun and sun every year and provides Spain and her people with much-needed pesetas. As with property, one gets a lot of fun for one's pesetas.

What does make the hackles rise, however, are English snobs who say 'We don't much care for Spain' when they have explored no further than the beaches and English pubs of places like Torremolinos. Spain is a vast country, with something for every taste, both on the mainland and on the Balearic and Canary Islands. There is history beneath every pebble. You may abhor the bull-fighting but there is no denying the excellence of the wine, the food and the weather. The cost of living in Spain, though not so attractive as it was, is nevertheless quite attractive, especially away from the Costa del Sol. Electricity is not cheap, but with luck you will not need to use very much - a fire of almond logs in the winter is infinitely preferable to electric radiators anyway. Some meat is rather expensive, but fish, fruit and vegetables, as well as local wines and spirits, are cheap.

Although we have already said it, do use the professionals when buying in Spain. Your British selling agent, if not qualified himself, should be associated with an official Spanish agent who belongs to the Colegio Official de Agentes de la Propiedad Inmobiliaria. Allow about 10 per cent of the purchase price of your new home to cover the costs; these roughly are 6 per cent IVA (VAT), plus 3-4 per cent for notary and land registry and 1 per cent for a Spanish lawyer. IVA is higher (12 per cent) on building plots and commercial premises. If the time comes to sell you will probably have to pay again about 10 per cent to the selling agent who represents you, as well as paying the *plus valia,* which is a municipal capital gains tax. If the vendor does not pay this *plus valia* tax, the buyer will become liable. So check when buying exactly who is paying what. The taxes are not excessive but they do have to be paid.

Whereas in some countries the advice is 'don't get ill', Spanish hospitals and doctors are good. If you are intending to live in Spain and you are receiving a UK retirement pension (which together with increments will be paid in Spain) you may join the Spanish National Health Service, which covers almost all your likely needs. However, it is as well to keep up your private medical insurance premiums in case prolonged post-operative or geriatric treatment is necessary.

If you are seeking no more than a holiday home then the questions of status and income tax do not arise. If a more permanent arrangement is foreseen, consideration may have to be given to both these vexing points. However long your stay in Spain, you will be liable for Spanish tax for any income received or arising from work or investments in that country. If your stay there exceeds 182 days out of the 365, then your worldwide income will be taxed, for you will be considered a resident (a tax year in Spain is the ordinary calendar year). Here again professional advice will probably be needed, for Spanish tax forms are designed to vesicate the writing hand, or seem to be. There may also be a local income tax surcharge, depending upon where your home is, though at the time of writing this unfair imposition is being tested in the courts. The tax, where it is charged, is regarded as a licence to milk the rich by some of the greedier or more deprived local authorities. Having said that, the tax is not particularly high, but I firmly believe that income should be taxed no more than once.

One can stay in Spain for three months with just tourist status after which it would be necessary to cross the border to get your passport stamped, possibly having to remain outside the country for a full day before returning. Thereafter one can apply at the local police station for a *permanencia*, valid for a further three months; this can then be renewed. You will have to be able to show a reasonable income and that you have somewhere to stay. It will also be necessary to produce your passport, bank certificate, two passport photographs, plus stamp and government certificates *(Papel del Estado),* available from most stationery shops and post offices. For permanent residence, and full entitlement to health services, pensions and other benefits, it is probably better to apply for a residence permit, *Tarjeta de Residencia,* which is normally valid for one year.

Your Spanish lawyer will advise you on the procedure for obtaining your *residencia,* but having once got it there should be no difficulty renewing it every year, provided you do not blot your copybook! In certain circumstances the duration of the permit can be extended to five years. The initial application will have to be accompanied by a passport, proof of registration at the local British Consulate, two Spanish guarantors, the stamps and government certificates needed for a *permanencia,* four passport size colour photographs, bank proof of solvency, and the title deeds of your new home. In addition, a renewable entry visa from the Spanish Embassy in the United Kingdom will be required. Provided you receive your *residencia* there should be no duty on your home-contents when they are transported to Spain, but do give some consideration to the suitability of your existing furniture to a new existence in a different climate.

Final thoughts of a general nature. If you are moving to a large scale development it will, by law, have a community of owners (*communidad de propriedad*) who set the annual charges for maintenance of common areas. Have a good look at the terms of the agreement you are signing. If, on the other hand, you are building a shining new villa for yourself, do be sure to engage a reputable builder with a good and verified track record in your area. Study the written estimates carefully to avoid future bad feeling with your builder; he may, for instance, tender only for the building works, in which case you could hardly expect him to do all the electrical fittings or landscape the garden. It is quite normal to withhold the final 10 per cent of payment in case major defects manifest themselves during the first few months. Don't be too hard on the builder, however. Six months should be plenty of time to keep him waiting for what is, after all, his profit; and major defects would not, to my way of thinking, include hairline cracks in plaster or any other minor irritations.

Many people prefer to choose something older, even derelict. Bear in mind that Spanish building methods have only recently entered the twentieth century - sanitation may be somewhat primitive and electrical wiring will probably be at best risky and at worse unlawful. Another nasty thought... check that the previous owner had paid ALL property bills, water and electricity, for a new owner can be liable for these if he is not careful. When buying that remote hill farm, which despite the risks would be my own choice, you will at least escape the noise of the ubiquitous 'pop-pop' bikes and transistors, not to mention the people upstairs doing the paso doble. Spanish sound insulation between floors is not the best in the world, though again things are improving at some developments.

Getting away from the noise will also save money on community fees, but your own needs will have to be considered. If you want a private swimming pool, it will cost about £12 a week to maintain. Then there is the garden, but a local gardener can probably be found at reasonable cost. If all you are buying initially is a building plot there is no obligation to hurry with the construction of the building. You will receive an *escritura* (title), and when eventually you get round to the building, the *Notario* will draw up a new document, called *Declaración de Obras Nuevas.* Getting that vital title deed can take quite a while, several months sometimes, and do not forget that Spain, and France, virtually close during August. However, once the *notario* has witnessed the transaction, a copy

of the *escritura* can usually be obtained which should suffice as proof of owner-ship until the officially stamped document arrives. There are still some British owners who have never obtained an *escritura* to their property, and buying from them can be complicated. It involves the vendor appearing before the *notario,* or the Spanish consul in the United Kingdom, and making a formal declaration, renouncing ownership. Further complications can arise when the new owner seeks title to the property if he did not buy the property in *pesetas* in Spain (i.e. he paid the previous owner in pound notes in Great Britain). Better to avoid these situations if at all possible, though I am sure there are some splendid bargains to be found if you are brave. At least when buying an ancient property there should be no problem about proving its legality - in some parts of Spain investigations have shown that many relatively new properties were built ille-gally, and there is even a black market in forged documents. So that lawyer, well versed in Spanish matters, is absolutely vital.

In recent years I have visited most parts of Spain, but I have hardly scratched the surface of this expansive country. Let us now consider a few of the better-known regions; first the most southerly, so far as the mainland is concerned, the Costa del Sol.

Costa del Sol

It was not so many years ago that Spain's southern coast was first discovered by tourists. But now many of the 43 million annual visitors to Western Europe's second largest country head for the south, where some 320 days of sunshine are recorded every year. Like much of the coastline in Spain, this warm southerly area has a backdrop of mountains - indeed the country's average height above sea level is one of the greatest.

In many ways it is more similar to North Africa in climate, too hot for good wine growing (save for some very sweet liquids and the sherries produced further to the west), but ideal, when the rainfall does arrive, for growing a wide range of exotic fruit. The rain did finally fall on the Costa del Sol, ending three years of near-drought a few years ago and annual falls have since been back to normal.

The town of Marbella is now synonymous with the Costa del Sol, boasting a 'Golden Mile' of developments which are beginning to rival the Côte d'Azur in price, and popularity. After all, how many places are there in the world where one can swim before breakfast, play a chukka or two of polo before lunch, and (after a brief siesta), drive up into the mountains for an evening session on the ski slopes? There is something here for all ages and all tastes - there is even an entire development close to Marbella called Las Palmeras de Bena Vista which is specially designed for the over-50s, and the units are intended to make life easier for them especially should they ever become immobile.

One reason for the growth of popularity of the Marbella area has been its ease

ASHTON HILL, BOND
————————— SOLICITORS —————————

Ashton Hill, Bond have an established branch office in
Marbella on the South coast of Spain. For some years
now we have been associated with leading Spanish
lawyers in Madrid and Marbella.

We can offer a legal service on English and Spanish law,
such as the conveyancing of residential and commercial
property, company formations, commercial agreements,
wills and litigation in both Spain and the U.K.

For further information please contact our principal office
at Pearl Assurance House, Friar Lane, Nottingham
(telephone 0602-476651) or our Spanish speaking
English Solicitor in our Marbella branch office
(telephone from U.K. : 010-34-52. 77.82.90).

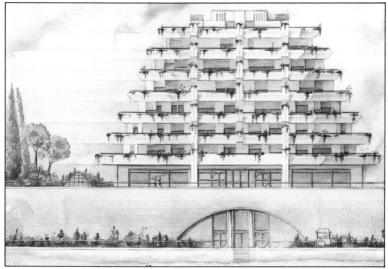

Sturgis have been appointed sole agents outside Spain for an exciting new development

MARBELLA EXCLUSIVE

Sturgis International has long believed that Marbella is **the** place to be when looking for a holiday or retirement home in the sun.

We are delighted to announce that we have been appointed sole agents outside Spain for one of the most important and prestigious developments being undertaken in Marbella.

Los Cipreses will provide exclusive apartments and family accommodation, close to the Hotel Don Pepe. Two complexes will also house commercial offices and shops, thus creating a thriving, self contained community of the very highest standard. Also the Club Nautico will offer the best and most exclusive leisure and business facilities on the coast.

The developers are the national Spanish company Club Financiero Inmobiliario, who have many years experience of developing such projects and who are fully backed and guaranteed by major Spanish finance houses.

Four buildings will make up Los Cipreses de Mar with Mare Nostrum closest to the sea and fronting directly onto the beach. Here 48 exclusive apartments will be built, having the benefit of the Club Nautico which includes a large swimming pool with an 80 metre poolside balcony overlooking the sea, set in its own garden.

The Nayade, Nereida and Poseidon buildings will complete Los Cipreses del Mar and will comprise 66 residences, each elegantly designed and styled to take the best advantage of the surrounding gardens and magnificent view.

Just across the Avenue Ricardo Soriano you move into one of the most exclusive residential areas of Marbella and here Los Cipreses will be built, containing residences which vary in size from one to five bedrooms.

Marbella has seen many developments over the years but the work by Club Financiero Inmobiliario will set a standard not previously seen. For full details contact Sturgis International in London or our Marbella office, 5, Avenue de Arias Maldonado, Marbella.

**140 Park Lane,
London WIY 4DN.
Tel: 01-493 1693**

**5 Av de Arias Maldonado,
Marbella, Malaga, Spain.
Tel: Malaga 777090**

An Englishman's Castle

in Spain

Buying A Home Abroad

Buying a property overseas can be a rewarding experience. The formalities however, can become tedious and take the edge off the excitement. The Bachmann Group can take care of these problems for you and explain the benefits of Company Ownership and, with the support of legal and technical advisors, achieve a secure ownership structure.

Together with a major U.K. Clearing Bank, we can offer loan facilities of up to 70% secured on the shares of the property owning company. Loans are available for up to 20 years in any major currency at 2% over base rate in the case of sterling, and 2% over 3 month LIBOR for other currencies. The loans are available to finance stage payments.

of access *via* Malaga's over-worked airport. However, some 16 years after General Franco slammed shut the gates of Gibraltar, the battered green portals are open once more providing travellers with an alternative access to the south coast. There are daily flights from Gatwick, sometimes two. The opening should have a significant effect on nearby developments like Sotogrande, a 1618 hectare (4000 acre) complex of golf courses, luxury villas, polo fields and one of the largest marinas in the Mediterranean. Wherever one stands on Spain's southern coast you can bet that someone, somewhere, is planning a marina for it, but this one really is taking shape. Nearby on the same estate, next year (1989) will see the opening of Centro Sotogrande, the largest residential and leisure complex on the coast.

There are now several marina developments along this southern stretch of coast, some started from scratch and others which have been built around an established fishing harbour. One of the first was Puerto Banus, close to Marbella, which still attracts the trend-setters. Several have tried to imitate and improve upon Snr Banus's fine creation, but not all have been successful - some have even suffered from problems with silt. This should not be a problem at Puerto Sotogrande; about 53 hectares (130 acres) were set aside for the project and a large proportion of the early expenditure on the outer port was taken up by the construction of the massive breakwater. I have watched this project from the early stages, and very much want to see the final tile put on the last house, although that might not be until the turn of the century. By then, we are assured, the massive port and marina will host 1500 yachts, some up to 50 metres (55 yards) in length, and about the same number of town houses and apartments. Sotogrande is only about 20 minutes drive from Gibraltar. It is also within easy striking distance of some pretty inland towns and villages, including one of my favourites, Casares, a little place with white houses clinging like limpets to the hilltop. A steep climb to the ruined abbey at the top is rewarded with breathtaking views, and guaranteed glimpses of eagles and vultures in flight and nesting on the crags below.

There are so many developments along this coast that it is perhaps unfair to single out any one to recommend. One of my favourites is a development of Spanish-style town houses on a former sugar plantation right beside the sea near Estepona. The site is called Villacana and was chosen by Barratt Multi-Ownership, the time-share arm of the house building giant, as its first toe in the water abroad. The development, with its sports facilities and beachside location, has proved a winner with British buyers, both for outright purchase and now also for time-sharing.

Beside the Don Carlos Hotel (formerly the Hilton) almost within jogging distance of the eastern end of Marbella, is Las Golondrinas, an expensive development of villas and apartments rejoicing in some of the best landscaping on the coast. The gardens, with streams, waterfalls, tropical trees and shrubs,

cost about £700,000 to create. It is also right beside the sea. As with most Spanish developments, prices have risen in recent years but because of the relative weakness of the peseta, in real terms, they have remained fairly static. Even so apartments at developments like Las Golondrinas (the Garden of the Swallows) cost between £50,000 and £200,000 or more to buy. An interesting architectural feature of this development is the ledges to help the swallows to nest. Eventually there will be no fewer than 19 swimming pools, and for people who prefer golf there are six courses within easy reach (though these are no longer so cheap to play on as they were). It also has one of the best tennis complexes on the coast, with well-known professional coaches.

Close to the elegant Marbella Club and the Hotel Puente Romano (with its own magnificent tennis complex hosting many international events) is a turning beside the new mosque which leads to a development called El Ancon Sierra. This is a ten-acre village which is being built by an Englishman, Mr John Green, and is located close to the many domed palaces belonging to even wealthier Arabs. The villas, with grand staircases, huge balconies, gardens, swimming pools and large fireplaces are, as you might expect, rather expensive, rising to around £500,000 for the best.

There are, of course, many developments which are much cheaper up and down this coast. There are excellent opportunities for investment around Nerja, for instance, east of Malaga, and numerous more reasonably priced apartments in developments on the north side of the coast road.

There are many British property owners in the Costa del Sol, who together with many other foreigners, including a lot of exceedingly wealthy Arabs and Japanese, are pouring much needed funds into Spain's coffers and helping solve her serious unemployment problem. Standards of building and design are now extremely high. Among the many worth seeing are Dominion Beach, Casas del Senorio de Marbella and, another of my favourites, the quaint Puebla Aida, where prices start at £45,000. All are within a day's drive of the Doñana National Park, 100,000 hectares (200,000 acres) of natural wilderness at the mouth of the River Guadalquivir. A day there, with a bottle or two of Manzanilla, is a naturalist's dream.

Country properties

Many Britons have sought the tranquillity of the hills above the noisy coastline. One Spaniard I met described the coastline around Marbella as *'de bote en bote'*, which loosely translated means cramped. Up in the hills one is never cramped, other than by a choir of insects.

Village houses and derelict farms still abound, not just in the south but across the whole of this vast country. Here proud old men with unsmiling faces sit, straight backed, observing the world, oblivious to the changes that are occurring elsewhere. Their wives in regulation black costume sweep around them.

Up here in the hills is real Spain, unlike the new Marbella and Torremolinos which are about as Iberian as Blackpool!

On the road to Jimena de la Frontera, and in the villages close to beautiful Ronda, there are village houses and farmhouses, some derelict and some ready to live in. A firm called Fincasol, with offices in the United Kingdom and Marbella, has made something of a speciality in these country properties, whilst taking care not to neglect the easier living on the coast. Customers fall into two main categories - those seeking a 10-to-15-acre 'hobby' farm, producing just about enough income for the holding to be able to 'wash its face', as agents say, and those serious expatriates who are looking for a land investment of 200 acres or more.

One can pay as little as £100,000 for a small hill farm with a little house which would require modernisation. The first rule is don't be afraid to haggle. Larger farms with good grade irrigated land, sell for £500,000 upwards. Avocados have not been too successful here.

Costa de la Luz

This area is dominated by Cadiz, ancient even when Julius Caesar had dreams of an empire. Cadiz has seen many eras: Punics, Romans, Visigoths and, more obviously, Arabs, with legacies which we can see. Nearby is Jerez de la Frontera, where the amiable Domecq brothers showed me with pride the *bodegas,* offering tastings of near-undrinkable but still alive 300-year old sherry and exceedingly drinkable 150-year old samples. The British firm of Harveys also has a show place *bodega* with ample sampling glasses.

Even the opening of Gibraltar leaves this coastline relatively inaccessible. The journey from Seville along the main road is reasonably fast, but monotonous; better by far to use the small by-ways, past fields of sunflowers nodding and smiling a welcome. Closer to the Portuguese border, near Huelva, is Europe's premier nature reserve 1166 sq km (450 sq miles) of wilderness between the sea and the Rocio Marshes called the Doñana National Park.

By the coast south-east of Cadiz, there is a 202 hectare (500-acre) development called Roche Residential which is within another nature reserve. This development is proving popular with British buyers, especially those seeking a gentle and quiet retirement. The area which contains the development is the 1214 hectare (3000-acre) Icona Nature Reserve, bounded by a small river. The campers are well away from the grand villas that are being build by Roche. The area is within an easy drive of Chiclana, famous for its fino sherry; and also close to Puerto Santa Maria, which has a casino and the largest bullring in Spain. Plots are sold by the metre at Roche, and prices vary enormously according to where they are. Some people have bought more than one. The development includes a club house and a huge communal swimming pool, but most people also have a pool of their own. The climate here is mild in winter and beautifully warm in

Woodside Europa

PAULINE BOLTON specialises in 'EXCEPTIONAL HOMES" on the most beautiful and exclusive part of the COSTA BRAVA, 40 miles from France, and in the lush green countryside of CATALUNYA, where the QUALITY OF LIFE IS SECOND TO NONE.

Our portfolio of resale properties contains examples of superlative coastal properties, some on the waters edge, and others overlooking the Mediterranean. Superbly restored ancient country houses and estates and beautiful village houses are also offered exclusively.

May we "share the secrets" contained in our portfolio and introduce you to lifestyle and ambience of CATALUNYA, which we know so well.
telephone Pauline Bolton - 0284 84 743 and 8855

WOODSIDE EUROPA LTD.,
INGHAM,
BURY ST. EDMUNDS,
SUFFOLK, IP31 1NR

GIBRALTAR AND THE COSTA DEL SOL'S LEADING ESTATE AGENT

IS NOW IN THE UK

Our staff are available to give you advice on

- ★ **A WIDE RANGE OF NEW AND RESALE PROPERTIES**
- ★ **INDIVIDUAL BUILDING PLOTS**
- ★ **PROJECT MANAGEMENT OF CONSTRUCTION**
- ★ **A LARGE SELECTION OF FINCAS AND FARMLAND**
- ★ **LAND FOR DEVELOPMENT**
- ★ **VALUATIONS AND PROFESSIONAL ADVICE (API 496)**
- ★ **RENTALS AND PROPERTY MANAGEMENT**

OUR AREA IS FROM GIBRALTAR TO MARBELLA AND INLAND TO JIMENA.

Contact: PMS Estate Agents Ltd
TELEPHONE: (0628) 770011

Weir Bank, Bray-on-Thames
Nr. Maidenhead, Berks SL6 2ED

summer but is seldom, because of the Atlantic Ocean nearby, too fiercely hot. It offers a benign and pleasant life-style, but one which some might find boring after a while. I met one retired couple who said they wished they had moved there years ago, and another who secretly admitted to being 'bored stiff, but we don't want to admit we made a mistake!'.

Costas Brava, Verde, Blanca and del Azahar

The Spaniards always seem to be inventing new names for stretches of coastline, as if they were only just being discovered. Recently I revisited the Bay of Rosas for the first time in 12 years - how it has changed. Now Rosas is, or was, in the Costa Brava, but locals, feeling that they are a cut above the Costa Brava, have dubbed the coastline the Costa del Coral, coral coast. To be frank, there is not a lot of coral there but the snorkelling is rewarding.

It is one of those areas, rather like Cyprus, where developers are afraid to put a spade into the soil lest they smite some ancient monument. A great deal of holiday development has taken place between Rosas and La Escala, not all of it attractive. All the fun of the fair is there, the candyfloss rubbing shoulders with the culture, and neither seeming the worst for the experience. Close by are the fabulous ruins of Ampurias, founded by Greek traders around 575 BC and adopted some 800 years later by the Romans as a sort of holiday and rest camp for tired centurions.

Within a short drive of La Escala, one is transported to a different age, to towns that have not changed for centuries. There is Pals, with its unmistakable *torre de les hores* (bell tower), whilst around the bay is Figueras, with its Dali Museum; Figueras, together with the Ampurias, are among Spain's most visited tourist attractions. This area is renowned for sea food, for despite its package holiday image there are good eating places to be found ... there is junk food too, if you want it.

At and close to La Escala, there is a wide variety of holiday development going on, including one called Punta Romana, on the cliffs above the Bay of Rosas, looking towards Ampurias. Apartments here range between £21,000 and £41,000.

Close to Pals, between and beside the sea and the golf course, is a new development where prices for one and two bedroom apartments range from £19,000 to £31,000; villas cost £39,000. There were some fully-furnished, two bedroom apartments near La Escala for only £15,500, ideal for holidays and letting, while perhaps the best buy of all was at a development called Gran Sol. This development is not right by the sea but has views of it, and it does have splendid communal gardens and a swimming pool. The apartments range in size from one to three bedrooms, all have balconies (the top floors being especially large, with a barbecue), plus fitted cooker and hob. Prices are between £17,000

and £26,000. A garage adds £3000 to the price.

The coasts of the Costa Blanca and Costa Brava offer better swimming than that on the south coast. Try listening to Bach and Albinoni through a 'walkman' while sitting on a rock three fathoms down. Inland music of a different nature greets the visitor; the curious reedy sound of a 'tenora' and numerous other instruments never seen at the Proms drift down narrow streets on festival days.

People in this healthy area seem to live for ever, due perhaps to the strenuous communal dances called 'Sardanas', accompanied by the local orchestra, known as a 'cobla'. Happy children, even happier great grandmothers, and proud adolescents skip and strut around the streets on St Jordi's Day, patron saint of Catalunya; boys and girls wear red sashes, and exchange gifts of books and roses, for this is the Day of Lovers; not a little bubbly is consumed and the scene resembles something between a circus parade and the Children's Crusade.

This whole area demands exploration and the rugged coast is only a short drive away. Slight variations in property law exist - the buyer pays the 'plus valia', for instance. Here magnificent country houses (masias) can be found for anything between £50,000 and £3 million; most property has separate accommodation for visiting guests, and fruit and vegetables grow as if in the jungle.

Then there is the northern coast of Spain, washed by the Atlantic, known as the Costa Verde, while below the Costa Brava we have Costa del Azahar, the coast of orange blossom, and the Costa Blanca. The two former locations both offer a wide range of holiday and retirement properties which are a good deal cheaper than those in the south. One could be quite content in Las Fuentes, an area north of the old town of Valencia close to fertile farmland with manicured almond trees and citrus fruit. The whole area reeks of ancient history; on the cliff face on part of the Sierra de Irta range behind Las Fuentes are wall paintings almost as perfect today as when they were drawn 12,000 years ago.

Within Las Fuentes is a development called Fuentemar, with town houses and apartments costing around £16,000 and rising to nearly £30,000 for a three bedroom house. Nearby, an almond plantation has been divided into half-acre plots and two bedroom villas are being built for only about £25,000 all-in - one of the best bargains in Spain. Las Fuentes, started in 1967, has been treading water ever since the slump of the early 1970s but is now beginning to buzz again. The new 220-berth marina is also nearing completion, and berths are now being sold on a 42-year lease.

Below Valencia but above Alicante is the once-quaint Benidorm on Spain's east coast, with Jávea and Denia among the towns that always attract the eye of the British. Indeed, Denia probably has more historical links with Great Britain than any other town along this coast. From here, one can take a ferry ride for about £11 across to Ibiza. Denia owes its 100-year old harbour to Britain which established a prosperous trade in raisins. The town is dominated on one side by ruins of the ancient castle and on the other by the mighty Montgo, 2000-feet of

rock which rises sheer above olive and citrus plantations. It was from the top of this dramatic wall of stone that the Romans cast down wayward slaves and other people they disliked.

Close to where the unfortunate enemies of Rome must have landed, is the enormous Marquesa development. It all started more than 20 years ago when a tailor from Brussels, Tony van Stiphout, first built a small holiday home there for his mother. He realised the potential of the area and bought up wide tracts of land. The development which he has established there already has more than 1000 villas on large plots of land, and is attractive, both aesthetically and financially. A feature I liked was the built-in furniture rendered in the same style as the walls ... more comfortable than it sounds.

Another reasonable development, low in price but not in quality, is Gran Alacant, close to Elche, a friendly town famous for its excellent dates and its botanical gardens but avoid driving there when football matches are scheduled. From Gran Alacant one can see (but not hear) planes full of holidaymakers bound for nearby Alicante airport and Benidorm beyond. Views of the bay are excellent.

Gran Alacant is a 809 hectare (2000-acre) estate in the early stages of development. It was taken over about five years ago by the Banco Exterior de Espana, which is comforting for buyers to know, and is close to the interesting harbour of Santa Pola, where one of Spain's largest fishing fleets rubs shoulders with an armada of private yachts. I felt that some of the blocks of apartments looked rather stark when the bank moved in, but with clever landscaping they are now beginning to mellow into most attractive holiday homes. Below is a splendid beach, but there are, of course, swimming pools within the development and every apartment has a balcony. Prices started at not much more than £12,000 for a one bedroom unit and rose to about £30,000 for a four bedroom apartment. The strength of the pound against the dollar has encouraged more British visitors in the last year or so. More Europeans are also being wooed.

Still further south, on the way to Cartagena, is La Manga, a 14-mile long isthmus of sand, once used as a gun range, but now smothered with apartment blocks, some gruesome, some quite nice. The sleeve of sand shelters a 100-sq mile inland sea called the Mar Menor which is ideal for water sports and safe bathing. Because of the earlier bombardments there is nothing old on the strip of sand, and the casinos, bars and apartments may not render it suitable for permanent retirement, though as a straight holiday investment it is probably all right.

Nearby, on the mainland is the La Manga Club, in a 'saucer' of fertile land surrounded by a frame of mountains. It is a different concept altogether, and covers 1400 acres. La Manga is one of the first developments in Spain to offer what the Americans call the 'total leisure experience'. However, you are not obliged to play golf, or tennis, or any other sport for that matter, if you just want

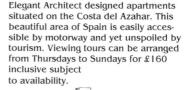
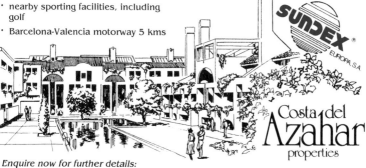

to sit by the pool.

La Manga has rather a chequered past. It all started when a shoe millionaire, Gregory Peters, saw his dream turn into reality in 1972. The development went the way of many of the kind when the Arabs changed the world in the mid 1970s, and the banks moved in during 1978. The golf had been successful enough, though the courses will be improved further, but the residential side of the venture had not proved popular. Finally in 1981 it was acquired by European Ferries for considerably less than the £10,000,000 it had cost Peters to create and now it has changed hands yet again. There is talk of adding another course to the two 18-hole championship courses already existing, and possibly even a fourth. Beyond the crescent of hills that frame this club is more than a mile of Mediterranean coastline on what is now dubbed the Costa Calida (the warm coast), though strictly speaking we are in the heart of the Costa Blanca.

The development offers a wide range of properties, from aparthotel units right up to huge villas. It has to be said that there is a one and a half-hour drive from Alicante airport. The sports facilities are many and various, including bike tracks, riding, tennis, bowls, a health centre, and even cricket at the club's own Oval. There are also numerous opportunities for what Americans call 'water oriented' (sic) sports at nearby Mar Menor.

La Manga Club is one of the most ambitious schemes in Europe. If all goes according to plan, within ten years there will be a total of at least 2500 units of accommodation, more hotels, extra golf courses, and facilities for every age and taste. Especially attractive among the most recent developments is the village-style development called Bellaluz Village, built around a pretty square with fountains, shops and bars. Studios there start at below £20,000, with the larger apartments and penthouses rising to above £50,000. My guess is that La Manga Club provides for all human needs except one, curiosity - a car would be essential to explore towns like Cartagena and Murcia, and beyond into the remote and vast Sierra de Segura.

Balearic Islands

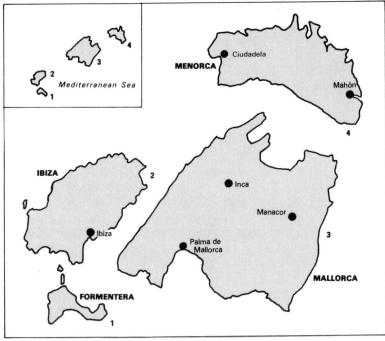

Mallorca, Menorca, Ibiza, Formentera and 12 other islands/islets

Capital of the archipelago: Palma de Mallorca, Majorca (Mallorca)
Population: 532,946
Area: 5012 sq km (1935 sq miles)
Average temperatures: High 20°C (70°F) Low 15°C (54°F)
Annual average rainfall: 347 mm (13.6 in)

One does not need 'O' level geography to claim a reasonable knowledge of this archipelago of enchanting islands. Mallorca, to use its correct spelling, Ibiza and Menorca have, in recent years, become honey-pots for swarms of tourists. Needless to say there are large areas which are now anything but enchanting, but fortunately development of hotels and cheap apartment blocks has been largely confined to areas beside wide beaches. If they have not actually been on holiday to one of the islands, most people will have at least considered doing so. Several million tourists visit Mallorca alone each year.

First impressions can be very misleading. My first visit to Mallorca was about 12 years ago on a package tour with small children to one of the man-made resorts along the enormous Arenal Beach, east of the island capital Palma. It was

Delightful & unspoilt

MENORCA

For Sale
Established **VILLAS** and **APARTMENTS** or **PLOTS** where we will build a villa to your specification.

Price range:- £20,000 – £200,000

Holiday Lets
2-4 bedroom villas and apartments adjoining beaches and bays, with pools if required.

We offer:

★ A genuine service if you are interested in acquiring or renting property.

★ Advice on annual costs, rates of local income tax, wealth tax, medical services, solicitors and any other query you may have.

★ Mortgage – available through an established broker in the U.K. or bankers in Menorca, subject to status.

Brochure and price list from:

awful, but a car ride to the west of this diamond-shaped island restored our faith as hairpin bends wound us through some of the most dramatic coastal scenery I have seen. The Torrente de Pareis, a massive canyon, was most rewarding of all. Mallorca is a large island, with nearly 300 miles of coast line; tourism steals only about 10 per cent of the island's charm leaving countryside and old towns and villages that are little changed since Frederic Chopin chose it with George Sand as the place to try to restore his frail health. Chopin's town of Valldemosa, although itself inevitably something of a tourist attraction, is unspoiled.

Half the resident population of 45,000 lives in the capital, Palma, a city not to be missed, with a magnificent cathedral. As with mainland Spain, the young workforce seeks the places where the tourists go, and so there are still opportunities for foreigners to buy village houses and run-down farm-houses. One agent told me that a derelict country house with no water or electricity but with a fine location, might still be found for £10,000. As always, consent would have to be sought before any serious alterations were undertaken.

The Mallorcan islanders themselves are proud of their independence, as indeed are the residents of all the Balearics. The group has its own parliament, with representatives of each of the four main islands meeting regularly in Palma. Mallorcans even perpetuate their own Catalan-like language, with two hours of it being taught in schools every week. There are some minor differences from the mainland in the laws concerning property ownership and laws of inheritance. There is a maximum area which a foreigner is allowed to buy (2000 sq metres (21,520 sq ft) in town and 5000 sq metres (53,800 sq ft) in the country), but joint ownership is permitted so the limit can be greater when more than one person is buying. Some people have formed a company to buy a property (such as a small farm) which exceeds the allowable space. Britons considering retirement there would have to show a reasonable income from pension and investment.

There are now some high quality developments springing up to help dispel Mallorca's 'cheap and cheerful' image of recent years. There is the exclusive Son Vide estate, close to Palma, with its 18-hole golf course, where villas can change hands for a million pounds or more. My guess, however, is that the 344 hectare (850-acre) Bendinat estate near Illetas, a rather boring suburb west of Palma, will become one of the most popular European spots within a few years.

Any lack of 'sizzle' in the immediate neighbourhood will soon be forgotten as Bendinat's development progresses. The first phase, of waterside houses, was sold before a brick had been put in position, and subsequent phases are promising to be just as popular. Several big names are involved in this exciting scheme, including King Fahd's brother, Prince Nawaf bin Abdul Aziz, who put up most of the money, and Prince Alfonso von Hohenlohe, creator of the Marbella Club, who will be host at the Anchorage Club, focal point of the development. However, the real coup is the employment of François Spoerry as the architect.

Eventually a total of about 2500 homes will be built, but completion is a decade or so away. The houses are being built in old Mallorcan style, with wooden shutters and pastel decoration, with pillars and archways built of stone from a recently revived quarry nearby. The outside of the units are charming and verge on opulent within. There is a small beach below the club and swimming pool, and 20 minutes gentle breaststroke brings one to an island bird sanctuary out in the bay. When one tires of the sea there will be plenty of landlubber activities, including the riding school and arena, a nine-hole golf course (possibly extended to 18 holes), a racquets club, health clinic, more than 50 shops, plus a bar or two. There are also plans for a retirement village, catering for the young at heart but slightly slower of limb. A ratio of one bathroom to each bedroom is being maintained throughout the development, and each unit has a working fireplace, essential on those cool Mallorcan winter evenings.

Ibiza

Ibiza, the second largest of the Balearic Islands, being about 25-miles long and 16-miles wide, has a capital of the same name which is head and shoulders above many of its rivals. Built on and below a dramatic hill crowned with a magnificent cathedral and castle, the old town has preserved much of its charm.

Sadly not all the island has been spared the awfulness of modern Spanish

development. The fields behind San Antonio have been left ragged with half-finished villas and apartment blocks scarring the once-lovely countryside. Every area, it seems, has its share of horrors, but fortunately there is still plenty of Ibiza left for us to explore and preserve. There are many faces to this island. There is the face that attracts 300,000 British tourists every year; then there is the more subtle face with persuades some of them to stay and set up home. There is a third face too, a craggy face, full of character, that endured savage injustice in the 1930s and the dictatorship that followed. It witnessed Spaniard killing Spaniard, and to me, this manifested itself in the countenance of an old lady sitting by the fortified church above the town of Santa Eulalia. She looked blankly through us when we spoke to her in English and then Spanish. She speaks only *Eivissenc,* a local dialect.

Ibiza is one of the 'Pine Isles', and like its little neighbour Formentera it appeals to people who like to be outrageous once in a while. Bathing costumes on the beaches of Formentera are about as common as unicorns, but some people do wear them on Ibiza. There are some elegant developments on Ibiza, including that at Roca Llisa, a 840 hectare (420-acre) development not far from Ibiza town with a golf-course and small beach. Alternatively, if the bustle of a marina is preferred, a local lawyer in Santa Eulalia is moving a mountain called S'Argentera (meaning silver mountain) lorry-load by lorry-load to the south facing shores of his town to build an ambitious 700-berth harbour for wealthy yacht owners. It took him several years to get permission, for these islands have at last realised that care must be taken with future development lest the very beauty people come to see is destroyed. Beside this grand marina low-rise apartments are to be built, all with sea views and balconies, but they are likely to be fairly expensive, starting at around £50,000. One could indeed be very happy in retirement - it is not so small as to induce what is known as 'island fever', a condition of bored contentment.

Menorca

Menorca's rival islands will tell you: 'The wind, she is always blowing there'. Last January, shirtsleeves rolled above the elbow, I could have been in Dorset in June; it all felt very English, and pleasantly warm. Occasional glimpses of Menorcan farmhouses, with distinctive green or brown shutters and some of last season's pumpkins still stored on the roof, reminded me that this was Spain.

This is an island that has appealed to generations of Britons. Indeed, for nearly 100 years, save for two brief periods when France pinched it from us, Menorca was a British possession; it was finally ceded to Spain under the Treaty of Amiens in 1802.

Much evidence of that occupation remains. The only major road, linking the capital Mahon and its amazing natural harbour with Ciudadela, the quaint old French capital, is still called Kane's Road, named after a popular and humane

MENORCA COUNTRY CLUB

THE FINEST DEVELOPMENT IN THE BALEARICS

PLAYAS DE FORNELLS
CENTRO DE-INTERES TURISTICO NACIONAL
MENORCA·SPAIN

A stunningly lovely, award winning design concept of prestigious apartments, garden houses and villas necklacing one of several crystal clear bays.

All lushly landscaped from our own nursery stocks. These select properties are ideal for holidays whilst also providing fine investment prospects.
The exclusive Country Club sports a vast pool, tennis, jacuzzis, gymnasium, etc.
Wonderful windsurfing and sailing. 2 golf courses nearby.
Please telephone for details, prices, colour brochures and videos.
Also for schedules of weekend inspection flights to see new 'front line' phases starting now.

MENORCA COUNTRY CLUB
Shepperton Marina, Felix Lane, Shepperton. Tel: (0932) 243104 / 243168

HOLIDAY - RETIREMENT - INVESTMENT

MAJORCA
COSTA BLANCA
MARBELLA
HACIENDA GUADALUPE
(between Estepona and Gibraltar)

SOUTH TENERIFE

We believe we have one of the most extensive selections of Overseas Properties presently on offer.

Contact for full details and service

William D. Hawthorne & Co

Estate Agents • Auctioneers • Surveyors
14 Waterloo Road, Wolverhampton,
telephone 0902.27257

proconsul, Sir Richard Kane.

Of the island's 55,000 inhabitants about 2,000 are from the United Kingdom, with many more owning holiday homes. Most describe it as England without the violence and extremes of weather. It can get windy, but not as often as the Mallorcans would have us believe.

Although package holidays can still be taken this is essentially a villa island; no new hotels are being built, and strict guidelines are imposed on new building, for style, colour and height ... two storeys being the limit.

Menorca boasts more than 120 fine beaches, many of them deserted, and more in fact than all the other islands in the group put together. It is a coast of islets, caves and natural harbours, carved by strong sea currents. Inland, the undulating green hills are criss-crossed with stone boundary walls and blanketed with wild flowers. It is hard to reconcile such rustic bliss with the savage events of its history, slavery and mass killing.

Menorca is famous for its gin and its cheese, the latter provided by some 25,000 resident Friesian cows. Once there was a thriving wine industry but, as in most of Europe, the vines fell victim to the dreaded phylloxera. The island also produces the most comfortable shoes and sandles of soft cowhide, one cobbler assuring me that his product was 'guaranteed for 5,000 miles'. Menorca was also the 'birthplace' of mayonnaise: during one of the brief French occupations the Duc de Richelieu's chef discovered the local 'salse mahonesa' being made by a local farmer's wife, from which today's rather inferior liquid is descended.

There is a Catalan-like Menorcan language, much influenced by those years of British occupation. Words like 'bottle' creep in to it. There is culture too, including a fine opera house (Spain's oldest) in Mahon, and a monastery (and bar) atop the island's highest point (the 363 m (1,190 ft) Monte Toro). A good selection of restaurants awaits the visitor, with fish the speciality, of course. Es Pla, by the sea in Fornells, and Rocamar, run by an opera singer in Mahon, are especially interesting.

Old farmhouses can still be found, needing restoration, as can town houses, but the latter are not cheap.

Property laws are much the same as on the mainland, but do check on minor differences concerning inheritance. There is a limit on the amount of land an individual can buy - 2,000 sq m (21,528 sq ft), but allowances are made for other members of the family. Some owners have formed a company through which to buy, bypassing this problem. The island has a development plan, with Green Zones vigorously protected. Flights are not as frequent as one might hope, but with that 'island fever' so easy to catch, most will not worry too much about that.

Canary Islands

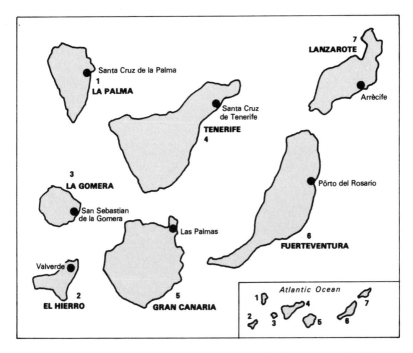

Tenerife, Lanzarote, Fuerteventura, Grand Canary, La Palma and other islands

Capital of the archipelago: Las Palmas, Grand Canary
Population: 1,170,224
Area: 12,084 sq km (4666 sq miles)
Average temperature: High 24.2° C (75° F) Low 17.8° C (64° F)
Annual average rainfall: 196 mm (7.7 in)

It seems almost an insult to attempt to dismiss this fascinating and varied group of islands in a few lines at the end of a chapter on Spain. Each of the seven main islands deserves a book to itself, and each in its way is worthy of consideration for holiday or retirement investment. They sit just above the Tropic of Cancer; the eastern island of Lanzarote, so loved by people whose joints are beginning to ache a bit, is only a short way from the African coast and the Sahara. All are the result of volcanic upheavals, the last not so long ago, and the greatest of which heaved the might Mount Teide on Tenerife more than 12,000 feet towards the sky. It is Spain's highest mountain, and if we were to ignore sea-level it is one of the greatest outcrops of rock to soar above the earth's crust anywhere in the world. The group of islands sits roughly on the Greenwich meridian, so it is usually the same time of day, if a mite warmer, as it is in London.

It can be like a perfect summer's day in Dorset. After matins at All Saints' Church, I joined the congregation for coffee in the vicarage garden, followed by a gentle game of tennis and croquet at the nearby club. Its slightly musty club-house is decorated with pictures of the Queen and her family when they were somewhat younger than they are today, and beside the noticeboard, littered with fixtures, is a table with neatly folded English newspapers. In the gardens marigolds and hydrangeas abound, but nearby tropical plants and a distant sapphire-blue sea betray the fact that this is not Dorset, but Tenerife, and the club is the 80-year old English Club in Puerto de la Cruz. Many Britons over the years have settled here, and the Georgian sash windows on some older buildings show that this is not a recent phenomenon.

Tenerife, more than 1000 sq miles in area and the largest of the group, was used in the eighteenth century to acclimatise the many plants being transported from the New World to the Old. The Gardens of Acclimatisation are a testimony to this, and some of the most attractive developments are close to them. One of the men involved in building apartments for foreign investors is Tony Yeoward, whose ancestors brought bananas to the island, still an important crop. They also hit upon the idea of cruising, as opposed to simply travelling. Their revolutionary ideas were the basis of a British television series about a shipping line. A 21-day cruise from Liverpool at the turn of the century, taking in Lisbon, Madeira and the Canaries cost six guineas (eight guineas for first-class). Travel is a little more expensive today, but these islands that are on the same latitude as Miami and the Bahamas are less than four hours from Gatwick.

Less than an hour's drive from the steaming heat of the banana plantations, those trees that 'walk' a little every year, is the pine woodland that so resembles Scotland, and the prairie-like landscape at the foot of the great mountain. The summit, reached after a two-hour scramble from a cabin, is one of the best places in the world from which to watch the sunrise if you are adventurous enough to make the journey. Up here one can ski, while on the beaches far below children can play by the sea all day without getting chilled. Even in winter the sea is seldom below 21°C (68°F).

East, past Gran Canaria with its capital Las Palmas and scenery that ranges from moon-like plateaux to luxuriant valleys, is Fuerteventura, second largest of the islands, arid in parts but possessing uncrowded sandy beaches. Nearby is Lanzarote, and its little neighbour La Graciosa, strangest of all the islands.

Lanzarote's volcano, Timanfaya (fire mountain) still smoulders, and chefs use its breath to grill steaks for tourists: those that have not had heart attacks after a massive water spout created by a mischievous guide has roared into life. There are no green meadows or rushing streams on this island, indeed one might be forgiven for thinking that the pilot had landed on the moon by mistake.

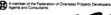

But there are greys, blues and pinks, dramatic dust that bursts into life after one of the rare showers. The soil is fertile but as nature has not been bountiful with her rainfall, water has become liquid gold. Little walls are built around crops to capture and preserve moisture, and desalination plants are helping to cope with the demand imposed by tourists. Gardens have colourful plants with lawns of *picon* (volcanic clinker) which are raked, not mown. The picon helps preserve the moisture. Wise villa owners have a well to store waste water for irrigating their gardens. A huge area of the island was covered by jagged black lava during six years of intense volcanic activity between 1730 and 1736. Although 36 new craters were formed not a single life was lost. Nothing grows in this part - it is the devil's own garden.

Despite its thriving tourist industry there remains a delightful innocence. Fishing villages with excellent local food are easy to find, and even the local wine becomes palatable after a few glasses. Old women still harvest the tiny white cochineal beetle that hides in the opuntia (prickly pear) cactus. It is now the only place where this is done. Among the tourist attractions are some amazing caves where, if you are lucky, you may hear a Baroque concert - if you go to the other caves you will be assailed by disco music, but a compensation is an underground lake with unique blind crabs that seem not to mind the decibels.

There are several time-share developments on Lanzarote and Tenerife, including some built by our own British building group, Wimpey.

Other islands are the 1184 sq km (457 sq mile) La Palma, with its massive crater 27 km (17 miles) in circumference. It is a complete contrast to the arid Lanzarote, being very green; then there is the mountainous Gomera, from which Colombus sailed for the Americas, and finally the most westerly island of Hierro, with dramatic cliffs and steep beaches but fertile land among its 433 sq km (167 sq miles).

Among the most popular Canary Island developments currently taking shape is the Golf del Sur, well away from Los Cristianos. Here there is something for most tastes and pockets, and a superb commercial centre with a street full of unusual restaurants is nearing completion. For someone seeking just a holiday hideaway (with rental return) the excellent Parque Don Jose, near Las Galletas, would fit the bill. Prices start at just £26,000.

In addition, for the more adventurous, there remain some delightful abandoned farmhouses in the cool of the hills. They will probably have a well (*pozo*) but if not a reservoir, called a *charca*, will have to be built for about £3000. Getting power to the house could cost anything between £100 and £10,000. Water, piped in open ducts, costs £15 for a delivery of 25 pipas, a pipa being five cubic metres. Prices for ruins start at about £10,000, but avoid property more than 900 m (3000 ft) above sea level, for it can get cold; grapes and other fruit grow well up to that height too. It is prudent to seek local advice, and take care to build in keeping with the vernacular and no more than 186 sq m (2000 sq ft); rural property

should retain 1 hectare (2½ acres) of land.

My favourite island of this group is Gomera, a fifth the size of its neighbour Tenerife, with dramatic mountains draped with a lichen-covered rain forest that is one of the most important ecological sites in the world. The terrain is so rugged that local farmers developed a whistling language, to communicate across the jagged ravines, called 'barrancos'.

The drab capital of San Sebastian nevertheless has one of the most romantic of Spain's paradors (government owned hotels) on cliffs high above the port. It is a good place from which to go house hunting. The opposite side of the island, if you have the stomach for some awesome hairpin bends on the way, is the most beautiful, with the Valle Gran Rey the most outstanding jewel.

All this innocence and beauty could soon disappear for a major shipping company has bought large tracts of land, alienating the native farmers who had depended on the water supplies, and generally threatening to spoil the little heaven by putting in a motorway, airstrip and massive hotels. I for one hope they fail, preferring the few harmless hippies and resolute travellers who are currently the only outsiders to venture there.

Here it is difficult to be precise about prices, for in recent years they have been rising sharply, in some cases as much as 16 per cent each year. There are still studio apartments available for around £35,000. Lovely though they are, I do not think they are everybody's cup of tea for a permanent habitation - it takes a special kind of Robinson Crusoe to live on a remote island. Many have found them perfect for that 50-50 sort of arrangement, six winter months in Lanzarote and six summer months in Suffolk, at least for the first few years.

If a week or two of time-sharing is wanted, as a sort-of stepping stone to something more permanent, then they can be had for between about £1500 and £3900, according to the size of the unit and the time of the year.

St Lucia

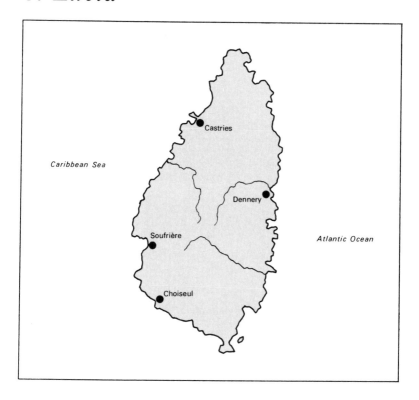

Each Caribbean island is deserving of a book to itself, but St Lucia could fill an encyclopaedia. Visitors are assured a welcome rather better than that received by 67 Englishmen whose ship Orange Blossom was blown off course there in 1605. They were made to feel welcome enough, but within a few weeks less than 20 remained alive.

The island is a mere fingernail west of Barbados on your atlas. There is plenty on which the millionaires can indulge themselves, but there are also large areas of unspoiled wilderness for the likes of me. The slash and burn agriculture has been stopped, so the beautiful coral reefs that shelter the island from the raging Atlantic are not engulfed with silt running off the fragile land.

This tropical paradise has been at the centre of a tug of war between France and Britain since the 16th century; its main language is English, but there are some who still speak the strange French patois. Tourist attractions include the 'drive-in' volcano, but there is much more to the island than that. Castries was the only place one felt any resentment, for there is much poverty here. In this, the capital, a visit to Rains Bar, one of the few remaining colonial buildings, is absolutely vital; a meal there is always good value, but beware some of the cocktails, especially the Reverend's Downfall.

The people charged with shaping the future of this, the second largest of the Windward Isles, have to find the right balance between tourism, which accounts for half the income, banana production (some of the tastiest in the world), manufacturing and oil storage and refining. Fortunately the active St Lucia National Trust is looking after the island's natural resources.

Large areas are being preserved as natural rain forest, sheltering the now rare St Lucia parrot (the island's emblem). The best area for holidays and retirement is the south west, close to Soufriere and the Pitons, two sheer mountains that soar from the blue sea. Here Dr Dolittle was filmed, and here the Anse Chastanet Beach Hotel and time-share lodges await. A Canadian is building excellent houses here for British and American investors.

Building costs are quite high; government permission has to be sought if more than five acres are wanted. The coastline is protected by the Queen's Chain, a limit on building that protects a strip of land 53m (176.5) feet from the sea; this was deemed 50 paces of the king, and consent for development has to be sought and bought from the government. You get a lot of house for your money here, between £50,000 and £100,000 buying a very nice home.

Dominica

Dominica, named because it was discovered on a Sunday 500 years ago, is the largest of the Windward Islands of the Lesser Antilles, covering 290 square miles of rugged and beautiful terrain with a population of only 85,000 (25,000 fewer than Grenada). Plots of land are being offered around Soufriere (meaning hot springs) at the southern tip of the island.

Deep forests on the lower slopes of 5,000 foot mountains hide waterfalls and 350 small rivers. Two hurricanes all but wrecked the capital, Roseau, and the banana plantations, but things are getting back to normal. Those who retire there enjoy exemption from tax on income earned abroad. There is no capital gains tax, but a property transfer tax (stamp duty) of four per cent is charged, buyer and seller usually sharing the cost.

Portsmouth, the second town of the island, has an especially beautiful harbour, close to fine beaches, and the more adventurous visitor can explore the mangroves on Indian River by canoe. Here one really can feel like Robinson Crusoe, and there are plenty of Men Fridays, God fearing and cheerful, to help if you get into difficulties.

St Vincent

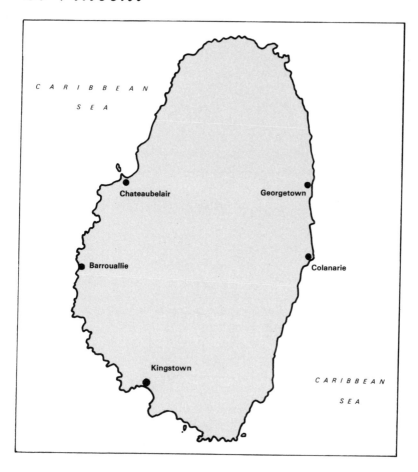

Status: Independent State
Currency: East Caribbean dollar
Capital: Kingstown
Area: 389 sq km (150 sq miles)
Population: 114,760 (1980 census)
Language: English
Longitude: 61°W   **Latitude:** 12°N
Average temperature: 26°C (79°F)
Annual average rainfall: 2921 mm (115 in)
Contact: The High Commission for the Eastern Caribbean States,
10 Kensington Court, London W8 (01 937 9522)

This island is part of the Windward chain and not far from St Lucia. St Vincent covers about 150 sq miles, which includes a mountain range and an active volcano, Soufrière, which last erupted in 1979. The island is the world's largest producer of arrowroot. The Grenadines, aligned to St Vincent, are known as the jewels of the Caribbean and are little more than islets that between them cover approximately 17 sq miles. They include the islands of Canouan, Mustique and Bequia, the latter has a time-share development of note. The house prices here, if land can be bought, reflect its exclusivity.

The eruption of Soufrière was a serious setback to St Vincent's progress for much of its agricultural land including several banana plantations, were destroyed. Gradually with the help of overseas aid, with some assistance given by the United Kingdom, things are returning to normal.

The general standard of housing for the islands' resident population is low, and since the eruption, the main thrust of government housing procedure has been to improve the sub-standard dwellings of the lower paid. Outsiders can buy property there but first must apply for a land holding licence. There is a two per cent stamp duty to pay on property purchase and this is usually shared between the buyer and the seller. Similar to St Lucia, there is no capital gains tax when selling.

Switzerland

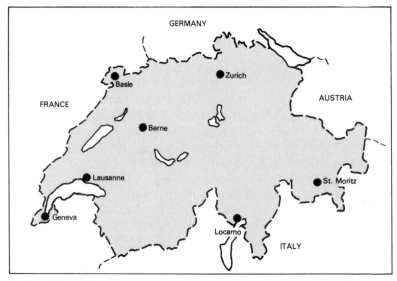

Status: Republic
Currency: Swiss franc

Capital: Berne
Area: 41,287 sq km (15,940 sq miles)
Population: 6,423,000 (1983)
Language: German/French/Italian/Romansch
Longitude: From 6°E **Latitude:** 45°N
Average temperature: Varied: 30°C/-15°C (86°F/5°F)
Annual average rainfall: 1232 mm (49 in)
International airport(s): 3; Geneva, Zurich, Berne
Contact: The Swiss Embassy, 6-18 Montagu Place, London W1H 2BQ
(01 723 0701/6)

One of the most attractive aspects of Swiss property is the continuity of style. Large apartment blocks tend to mirror and magnify the quaint hillside chalets, but beneath every cuckoo-clock building, large or small, is a huge concrete and steel cellar, euphemistically described as storage rooms. The Swiss are in a more or less direct line between Moscow and Miami, but they have every intention of surviving the holocaust; indeed they have to survive - it is the law. Regular inspections of these 'storage' rooms are made to check both water and food reserves, for these are nuclear shelters. Older buildings do not all have the shelters, of course, but if an owner wishes to alter or extend his property the local authority will require him to build one. Even a small extension to a hospital ward necessitated the medical officers commissioning the building of a 300-bed underground hospital with full operating facilities.

Perhaps it is because they have so much going for them: affluence, neutrality, wild flowers, and mountains, both for climbing up and for sliding down, that makes the life style so infectious. If you are hungry after a meal in a Swiss restaurant, even after the patron has forced a fifth helping on to your plate, you are unlikely to be charged.

It is very difficult for anyone who is not Swiss to get a foothold in this mountainous country, but only because its government wants to prevent property speculation. Indeed in 1984 a referendum that sought to outlaw the sale of any property to foreigners was only just defeated.

But every year the Swiss set a quota of sales. In 1980 it was 5000 but within five years the annual limit had dropped to 2000. Back in 1982 the limit for the whole Canton of Valais, which includes Zermatt and its Matterhorn, was a mere 300 licences. From January 1988, following a referendum in the canton, no further licences will be issued; something of a mad scramble is taking place to get the few remaining. The Swiss have imposed an absolute ban on the sale of property in commercial centres such as Geneva and Zurich, other than to Swiss nationals of course. For several years now the rules concerning resales have been strict. The lucky few outsiders who manage to buy one of the open market properties must retain it for a minimum of five years, and even then, it can be sold only to a Swiss.

However, as a local notary and praefect confided, the government is not an ogre. In extreme circumstances such as proven insolvency, serious illness, or of course death, the rules may be relaxed. Otherwise sale to another foreigner, after the five-year period, may be made only when it can be shown that every effort has been made to find a Swiss buyer. After ten years some cantons permit sales to non-Swiss without restriction.

Property in Switzerland, because of its scarcity and the remarkable strength of the Swiss currency, is, as you might expect, on the expensive side. However, as the Swiss franc gains strength against many other currencies, the relative value of the property shows considerable appreciation. Allow between two and a half and five per cent of the purchase price for legal and registration costs. This variance is because charges vary from canton to canton.

This is one country where a local loan will probably prove cheaper and preferable to one raised at home in the UK. Using the chosen property as security, a mortgage can be raised at interest probably not much more than six per cent. Most people, whether they buy a chalet or a small unit in an aparthotel, like to offset some of their expenses by letting when it is not in use. This letting should bring in about two per cent of the purchase price every year, perhaps more. Indeed, at an aparthotel where a return of four per cent is the norm, one is strictly speaking obliged to put the unit into the letting pool although the managing company can 'fail' to find a tenant if you really prefer not to have others use it. This two per cent income more or less tallies with the average annual outgoings, service charges, taxes and so on.

The purchase of property in Switzerland by a foreigner is normally for his own use as a second home, and strictly speaking, he is expected to occupy it himself for a minimum of three weeks every year. This rule is seldom enforced, but it is intended to discourage long term rental contracts.

For anyone proposing a permanent retirement in this land of affluence and mountains, the rules are very strict indeed. To stand any chance of being accepted an applicant must be of retirement age, over 60, and have no children under the age of 20. The application has to be made to the authorities in the chosen canton, and it is by no means an automatic procedure. Each canton has its own set of rules, but people seeking a residence permit must have considerable wealth in order to show sufficient income. Income tax *(impôt forfeiture)* is not assessed according to income in the way in which we are accustomed, but according to what each canton thinks should be paid. No forms or declarations are required, but a foreigner setting up residence in Switzerland could find himself paying perhaps 40,000 Swiss francs, perhaps as much as 100,000 Swiss francs, depending upon where he is living. It is simply the price you have to pay to live there. In the event of a sale, after the five-year minimum period has lapsed, any profit will be subject to a capital gains tax *(impôt sur les gains immo-*

bilier), although allowances are made for inflation and improvements to the property.

Prices vary and property around Geneva airport reflects its popularity; a chalet with three bedrooms, if you can find one on the open market, will cost from £250,000. Even a studio is likely to command a price of around £70,000 while one and two bedroom apartments range between around £125,000 and £150,000, or more.

The great joy of property in Switzerland is that people want to borrow it at most times of the year, for all the seasons have their own particular charms. This, coupled with the economic security, not to mention the shelter from the nuclear storm, puts Switzerland high on the list of desirable countries for investment, especially if you do not mind your money being locked up for five years or more.

Trinidad and Tobago

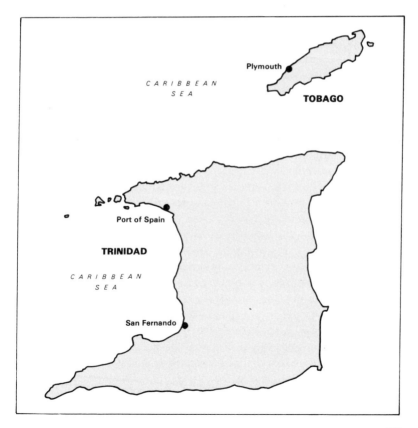

Status: Republic
Currency: Trinidad and Tobago dollar
Capital: Port of Spain
Area: 5130 sq km (1980 sq miles)
Population: 1,168,000 (1984)
Language: English
Longitude: 61°W **Latitude:** 10°N
Average temperature: 28°C (82°F)
Annual average rainfall: 1210 mm (48 in)
International airport: Piarco International Airport
Contact: The Trinidad & Tobago High Commission, 42 Belgrave Square, London SW1 8WT (01 245 9451)

They call Trinidad the land of the humming bird and the home of the steel bands. It is a large oil-rich island covering 4830 sq km (1865 sq miles); its much smaller but far prettier neighbour Tobago is only 300 sq km (115 sq miles). Trinidad is off the north-east coast of Venezuela. The islands gained their independence in 1962, with the government based in Port of Spain, Trinidad's capital.

Although a buyer's market currently exists on both of these two islands, foreigners are not being encouraged to move there. Any application for an alien land holding licence would have to be made through the Attorney General's office (c/o The Red House, St Vincent Street, Port of Spain). But fewer than a dozen licences are granted each year. The applications are received twice a year and to stand any chance of success the applicant must have proof of sufficient funds both to buy the house and then to live. They also need good character references and a good record of health; the application will also be more sympathetically received if there is a relative already resident on the islands. These rules apply even if the intended purchase is no more than a holiday home.

There are however some time-share developments worth considering, and there is a great deal of emphasis currently being placed on tourist related development. People lucky enough to get permission to buy will find that Trinidad and Tobago have a high standard of building, but property is not cheap. A bungalow at a seaside resort will probably cost more than £100,000.

Of the two islands, Tobago is the one well-worth considering. It is a beautiful little island with the most charming old English names for its villages and towns. After visiting this tiny island, you can see why the inhabitants want to try to keep it exclusively for themselves. If considering Trinidad then be careful where you buy seaside property as in places the water is not particularly appealing: the great River Orinoco, washes out a considerable amount of silt quite a distance from its estuary on the South American coast.

Turkey and Greece

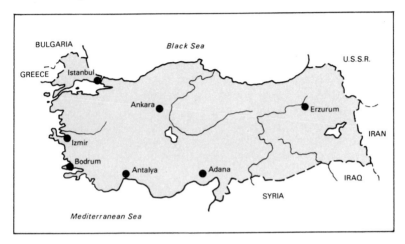

Geographically close, but politically poles apart, Turkey and Greece will figure prominently in our holiday and second home planning in the years to come. Greece is already a member of the EEC, and Turkey would like to join (despite opposition from her neighbour).

There are large areas of Greece where the sale of property to foreigners is forbidden; these are chiefly border areas which include many of those popular holiday islands, such as Crete, Corfu and those around Ios.

These restrictions however leave plenty of glorious places to consider. Especially beautiful is the area around Porto Heli, on the Aegean side of the Peloponnese, where Hapimag has one of its holiday developments. From there a short ferry ride brings one to the islands of Spetse and Hydra, where history and mythology merge.

An English-speaking Greek lawyer is essential, and the Bar Association in Akadimias Street, Athens, can supply a list. It is vital that funds for purchase are transferred properly, either through a bank or registered at the port of entry. Keep all receipts, for they will be required if you decide to sell up and return to England. Profit from a sale may remain locked up in your Greek bank account.

Some people get round this problem by selling to a fellow Briton before the Greek Notary Public at the London Consulate. Because of the problems of cash transfers most Britons with property in Greece keep their savings off shore, nibbling in to them when they leave the country. Allow between 10 and 12 per cent for property taxes and legal charges.

Access from Turkey to Greece is very tricky (although one can travel in the other direction all right). Both countries embrace the visitor with a warmth that

is rivalled only by the sun, but there seems to be little chance of the two burying their differences in the foreseeable future. The island of Cyprus has been covered earlier in this book under a separate heading.

Turkey is the flavour of the moment for people seeking new holiday destinations, and opportunities for purchasing a home there are growing all the time. A certain amount of faith is required, such as that which is said to launch one of the beautiful carpets into flight.

For the first time Turkey has a democratic government which is determined and strong enough to steer it into the modern world; it will have to overcome galloping inflation, put some tar on the roads and cope with an invasion of multinational tourists that will make the Crusaders look like a Sunday school outing.

Tourism still represents a relatively small part of Turkey's activity, more than half its 53 million residents still being employed in agriculture, but its growth is phenomenal. In 1987 nearly three million holidaymakers went there, about double the previous year's total.

Small wonder, when one sees the glorious coastline; it would be a tragedy if the sort of mass development which occurred in southern Spain two or three decades ago were allowed to ruin the very thing people visit this country for. Some of the Turks' own holiday developments, with serried ranks of little boxes, did not bode well for the future, but I gather the penny (or rather the Turkish lira) has dropped.

The mayor of Bodrum told me with pride of his town's plans to add 1000 tourist beds a year to the present 10,000, up to a maximum of 100,000. Fortunately this is a very large peninsular, but even so the number sounds rather high to me. The local authorities are also making determined efforts to eradicate the pollution of the sea by passing ships which has given rise to headlines about defiled beaches.

The town is imposing strict controls on building and British builders active in the area are having to conform with vernacular traditions which are not all to their liking. They include a limit of one square metre on window sizes, no building above two storeys, natural wood colours, a maximum floor area of about 108 sq m (1200 sq ft) and no flank walls longer than 6 m (20 ft) without a break. Log fires are encouraged but coal is forbidden. It is all in the name of conservation of character.

British developers currently getting started on projects in this corner of Turkey include Dean and Dyball Properties, proposing a vast marina project on 988 hectares (400 acres), and a modest but potentially beautiful development by Sunweald Properties beside the sea and below three ancient windmills on the north side of the peninsular. Prices, which include a furnishing package, start at £71,500.

The villas are being sold on a 99-year lease, which means that the land registry (*alim-satim vergisi*) charge is 0.3 per cent instead of the normal four per cent paid by both the buyer and the seller with freehold property. Stamp duty (*Damga Vergis*) and notary fee (*noter ucreti*) add a further one per cent to buying costs.

The procedure for property exchange is simple and efficient, and locals can complete a transaction in a day; it takes a little longer for foreigners, a couple of weeks perhaps, because central government in Ankara has to be notified. No one here bothers with lawyers, partly because the locals could not afford his services but chiefly because the notary's chief duty is to check that property is sold legally and free of any debts before title is granted. All property is clearly manifested in the registry (*'Tapu'*).

All property is subject to annual land tax charges, although some tourist developments are enjoying a five year tax holiday. This is like rates, and is assessed every four years. Owners will have no capital gains tax to pay when they sell, unless they own their property for less than one year. Money must be transferred through proper banking channels. A double taxation treaty is in the pipeline, but awaits ratification.

These are honest and hard-working people and so the absence of a guarantee of completion from the builder is perhaps not too worrying; however buyers should part with money only in stages, as work progresses.

The journey down to Bodrum from Izmir is somewhat arduous, but a closer airport is planned. On the way we stopped at Ephesus, the wondrous ancient city of wide streets and countless pillars; nearby are the remains of a tiny house where Mary, the mother of Jesus, is said to have died after her journey there with St John.

Bodrum itself is endowed with remarkable archaeological riches, both on land and in the transparent sea. Herodotus, the father of history, was born there in the fifth century BC. Halicarnassus, as it was named in his day, is also the site of the Mausoleum, one of the seven wonders of the ancient world, built by the greedy King Mausolus. An earthquake reduced it to ruins 15 centuries later, and some of the stone was used in the nearby castle built by the Knights of St John. Its gigantic scale can still be seen from the ruins today. In 460 BC Bodrum was ruled by Artemesia I, a lady of muscle given to beating up Greek sailors; she tolerated no male insubordination and altogether acted in a way which today would earn her the title of 'Iron Lady' - one felt one almost knew her.

Modern Turks still work the soil but television has entered the parlour; dubbing old westerns is big business. But many still spend winter evenings gathered round an indoor barbecue and singing to music provided by a 'saz', a seven-string elongated mandolin.

By day old men sit in bars playing 'Okey' and drinking raki, a sort of poor man's Pernod, but still the priests summon people to prayer several times a day from atop the minarets. Marriages are still arranged, but they normally work. Young girls are usually too busy stitching their carpets to go courting anyway; it takes them a year to embroider the 1,200,000 stitches in a square metre of carpet - small wonder we pay several thousand pounds for a good silk carpet with its tree of life and other designs.

Tips for unwary visitors include: 1. Toilet paper is found only in tourist hotels - Turks prefer to wash. 2. Land is measured in donums, which are 1000 square metres. 3. Be prepared for much kissing of cheeks, even though all Turkish men sport a moustache (biyik). 4. Hospitals are very good indeed, but everything has to be paid for. 5. Prisons are not so comfortable, and laws relating to drug pushing are exceedingly severe. Major crime still attracts the death penalty. 6. Plastic money has not really caught on yet; cash is preferred.

Visitors must remember they are entering a world that is very different from our own - a bridge between continents. The men are proud and handsome, enduring 'sunnet', that operation which is supposed to mark a boy's entry into manhood, and most women still wear the traditional baggy trousers (salvar) and shawl (esarp). You will be expected to enjoy a bout of camel wrestling when staying in the country.

Most towns have a loudspeaker system, for lost children, campaigns and the like. They tried a no smoking campaign recently - it didn't work; and be prepared to endure clouds of cigarette smoke in nightclubs and on the tourist class only Turkish Airlines. If you can get through the journey the rewards are unlimited.

Turks and Caicos Islands

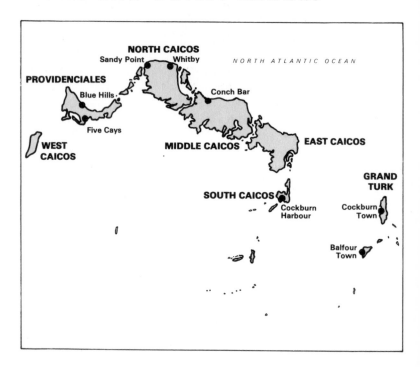

Status: British Dependent Territories
Currency: US dollars
Capital: Cockburn Town (on Grand Turk)
Area: 430 sq km (166 sq miles)
Population: 7436 (1980)
Language: English
Longitude: 71°W   **Latitude:** 21°N
Average temperature: 26°C (79°F)
Annual average rainfall: 530 mm (21 in)
International airport: On Providenciales Island - small airports on other islands
Contact: Foreign and Commonwealth Office, Whitehall, London (01 233 3000)

These two groups of islands, the Turks and the Caicos, some little more than cays or rocks, are separated by a 35 km (22-mile) wide channel. This deep stretch of water is called the Turks Island Passage. The islands are on the south eastern extremity of the Bahamian chain of islands and as one would expect, they have very similar weather conditions. Partly because they are a tax haven the flat and sandy islands are similar to the Cayman Islands of some 15 years ago, before property prices shot up.

As with most of the Caribbean islands, great emphasis is being placed on tourism, and there are a number of new hotels and holiday projects underway.

This British colony was, until recently, never in the news but since the drugs trade has sadly grown in America, these islands, like the outer Bahamian islands have become a convenient stopping over point.

Buying procedures, as one would expect, are not too dissimilar from those in the UK. Property above the price of US$5000 (which means virtually all likely to be considered by foreigners) carries a five per cent stamp duty. Legal charges start at around two per cent on cheaper property but reduce on a sliding scale downwards to half of one per cent in the case of very expensive houses. A wooden open-deck bungalow with three bedrooms, and built right into the rocks, would cost in the region of $62,500. There is no capital gains tax on the island.

West Germany

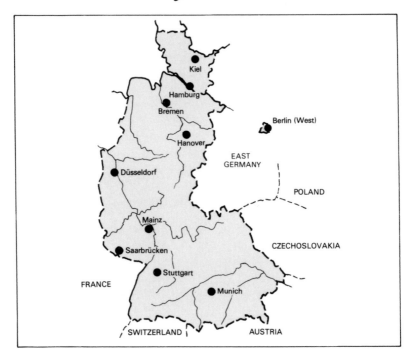

Status: Federal Republic (of)
Currency: Deutsche mark
Capital: Bonn
Area: 248,574 sq km (95,975 sq miles)
Population: 61,600,000 (1981)
Language: German
Longitude: From 6°E **Latitude:** 47°N
Average temperature: Varied: 18°C/3°C (64°F/36°F)
Annual average rainfall: 1077 mm (42 in)
International airport(s): 10; including Dusseldorf, Frankfurt and Munich
Contact: The Embassy of the Federal Republic of Germany, 23 Belgrave Square, London SW1X 8PZ (01 235 5033)

Building costs in Germany are exceptionally high, and as a result a surprising number of people are still forced to rent their homes. If the Germans cannot afford to buy a house, let alone a second home there, then houses are beyond the grasp of most Britons. Having said that, a healthy lifestyle can be achieved, particularly in a region like the Black Forest, the 90-mile tract that reaches south towards Switzerland. Especially popular for holidays are villages like Unterkirnach, and I did meet one English family who had settled there and were very happy indeed.

Personal taxation levels are not high, and there is no capital gains tax from the sale of property, unless the authorities deem the purchase to have been speculative. A five per cent property tax is collected when a house is bought, and for someone settling in Germany a wealth tax of half of one per cent a year may be charged on worldwide assets.

The best buys in the south of the country are undoubtedly the old village houses which Germans would say are in need of restoration (though British buyers might think them quite habitable as they are). These houses can sometimes be found for about £30,000, while new apartments, enormous by our standards, cost upwards from £40,000.

Germans do not like holiday homes standing empty for most of the year and so the sort of development that is available is the holiday village such as that close to the spa town of Bad Durrheim. Most of the 170 cottages sleep six, and cost between £35,000 and £45,000, but owners are initially allowed only one month's occupation each year, the remainder of the time being put aside for letting. However the owner does have an appreciating asset, together with a guaranteed income of at least £1500 per year.

United States of America

Status: Republic
Currency: United States dollar
Capital: Washington DC
Language: English
Contact: The United States Embassy, Grosvenor Square, London W1A 1AE
(01 499 9000)

It was only a few years ago that the pound in our pocket was worth 2.40 US dollars, and it seemed that every Briton with spare cash was seeking to invest it in a plot of land in Florida or California. Then suddenly it all changed. And not long ago we were even talking about dollar/sterling parity, though normality does seem to have returned for the time being. However, it really does not matter a great deal what the rate of exchange is, for land in the sunshine states of America seems set to continue to rise in value indefinitely. Those that bought in 1980 are luckier than those buying today. The reason for this price increase is that an awful lot of America's 230 million inhabitants are moving south, into what they call the 'sunbelt'. Whereas a few years ago they were looking for holiday or retirement homes there, nowadays the trend is for commerce and banking to move south, taking with it the young, well-educated and skilled American families.

Buying property in America is no problem, if you have the money. Using it for holidays is no problem, if you can afford to get there. Living there full time, whether for work or retirement, is not quite so easy. America does not easily permit immigration unless the applicants have very close relatives already living there. Work permits are hard to come by, unless your particular skill is desperately needed. Most people make do with an ordinary visitor's visa; alternatively application for status of resident alien can be made, but even this can take a year or two to achieve. Meanwhile the visitor's visa does suffice. Applications for the resident alien status are complicated, and success depends very much on the skill of your chosen lawyer (some are more skilled than others). The first step is to get a list of lawyers from the Florida Bar Association in Miami or from the corresponding association in San Francisco. As each state has its own federal laws it is wise to seek advice.

Owning a home in America neither hastens nor prejudices your application; most people retain a home in the United Kingdom as well, or at least until their status has been clarified. Sales of property involve the payment of a 20 per cent capital gains tax on profit, and if you earn money in the United States, or live there for more than 183 days in a fiscal year, you will be required to fill in one of the tax forms, but this task is not one for the faint-hearted amateur. Their tax system does differ considerably from ours. It reflects the ideals of the 'American dream'. Not only is the tax rate lower than ours but even the interest from your credit cards are taken into account when settling your yearly tax bill.

Britons will be able to draw their UK state pensions as well as their private pensions, but it is absolutely essential that private health insurance is taken out, and this must be adequate for medical expenses are very high indeed.

California

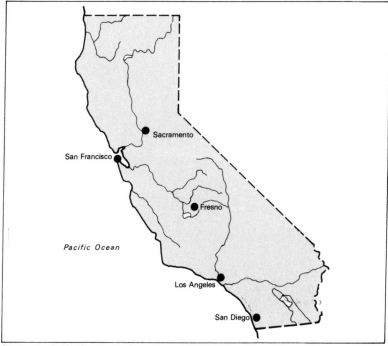

State capital: Sacramento
Total area: 411,015 sq km (158,693 sq miles)
Population: 24,724,000
Longitude: 114°W   **Latitude:** 31°N
Average temperature: varied
Major airport(s): Los Angeles International, San Francisco International

Most of the rules that apply in Florida also apply in California, although the state laws do differ. California is the fastest growing state in America, with property development growing faster than its other southern rival, Florida.

Although California's property development started well before the 1950s, its increase since then has been rapid. Most people automatically think of California as either Los Angeles (the 'capital' of the stars) or San Francisco. The latter has more character than the former. But California is a vast state and a very beautiful one. It embraces a rugged coastline and has many extensive sandy beaches. The hills and mountains are also very beautiful, and up here at times, it is hard to reconcile the fact that you are in the same state that produced Los Angeles. Here, as in Florida, nature shows that it has a lovely face.

Prices in California are higher than in Florida, approximately one-third higher, but again this depends greatly on the area. In the 'sought-after' areas in Beverley Hills, sumptuous residences exchange hands for many millions of dollars. Letting potential in California is great but naturally more to the many American visitors than to the British.

The architecture is more varied than that found in Florida, but this has as much to do with the terrain as it does with anything else. Houses are often very attractively set into the hill on which they stand. But you can still buy the traditional American-style ranch-house with three bedrooms or alternatively a 2000 sq foot apartment here. When you buy a home in either place, the price you pay will normally include fridge-freezer, 'stove' (not called a cooker in America), washing machine - and even a dishwasher! There are many new developments available in California, indeed, a few British developers are present here, notably Barratts.

Florida

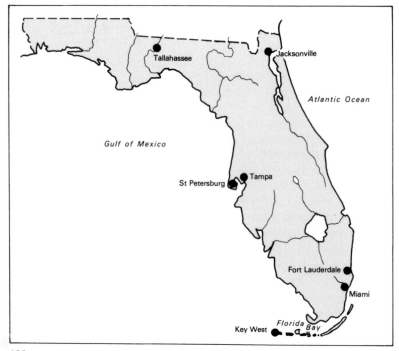

Capital: Tallahassee
Total area: 151,670 sq km (58,560 sq miles)
Population: 10,416,000
Longitude: 80°W **Latitude:** 24°N
Average temperature: 24°C (57°F)
Major airport(s): Miami International, Tampa International

The state most popular with Britons for holidays and at least partial retirement is Florida and it has experienced a phenomenal population explosion. In 1920 its residents numbered one million. By 1960 the figure was up to five million, and today it is well above 10 million. By the turn of the century it is expected to have soared to at least 14 million people. Every week more than 1000 people move to the sunshine state!

Hand in hand with the population explosion is a land-price explosion. Land near Miami which was selling for US$350 an acre in 1950 was commanding a price of US$100,000 an acre in 1980. When I visited the Deltona Corporation early in 1985, they were chinking glasses to celebrate the sale of 5600 acres at Tampa Palms for 38 million dollars - five years earlier they had turned down an offer of eight million dollars. The land of oranges, sunshine and the Everglades, has moved all too quickly into the twentieth century. Miami is fast growing into one of the major banking cities of the world, condominiums are erupting every-where, golf courses, tennis centres, polo fields, Disney World and a host of other 'leisure oriented (sic) experiences' are trying to cope with this rush to the sun. People still say 'have a nice day', and ask 'are you having fun?', and they mean it. A tasteless white concoction called 'grits', is still served with every meal, and no day is complete, it seems, without some 'dog and suds' (sausage and root beer). The language is punctuated with pitfalls, and please do not rest in the 'Rest Rooms'!

There is still abundant wildlife. Fishermen at Crystal and Withlacoochee Rivers still say they are half water and half wide-mouthed bass - so many fish, they say, that you can walk on the water! Man and wildlife seem to be cohabi-tating quite nicely in some areas.

It is a curious love-hate relationship that Britons tend to develop there. The life-style is infectious, the affluence unbelievable. Developments like Boca West and Wellington, where some houses have their own private aircraft hangers (some have double hangers), are a tribute to the 'American dream'. But where there is wealth there is usually poverty - do not get out of your car if you break down in Miami's Liberty City late at night. Palm Beach is where the incredibly rich people play. There is the magnificent Breakers Hotel, with beautiful ceil-ings and a wine list as thick as the bible. Men are arrested if they jog without a shirt on, and something approaching panic was caused when a tramp went to sleep on a seat in the main shopping street. People eat a lot as well. Enough food is thrown into the 'trash shute' every day to feed the rest of the world, or so it seems to me. It is a wasteful place, but it is their money that is being wasted. Many British people have bought a share of the fun and have quickly adapted to the lifestyle.

The range of property opportunities in Florida is great. I saw one house on Marco Island priced at seven million dollars, but the price did include its 1741 light bulbs! Luxurious 2500 sq foot apartments overlooking the sea command prices of around $250,000 in the more popular areas. Still on Marco Island (an acre currently costing one million dollars) and its neighbour Horr's Island (still being developed), named after Captain John Foley Horr, single-storey buildings have to be built 5 m (17 feet) above the high water mark in case of flooding. These attractive dwellings with their cedar shingled roofs cost around $80,000. It usually rains at 5 pm, but by then most residents are inside with their martinis. Beware the 35 mph speed limit - it is rigorously enforced.

There are a lot of developments in Florida, but just in time there is also an awareness of the need to fight for the preservation of nature. Beaches and mangroves are now protected by a Dune Act, prohibiting development close to the shore. One does not have to pay astronomical prices for a home in Florida, for building costs are not so high as they are in the UK. For $80,000 dollars one could find an excellent home, with 'walk-in' closets (wardrobes), fine communal swimming pools and golf and tennis facilities, giving a letting potential of perhaps 6000 dollars a year. While in Brandon, near Tampa, one can buy a two bedroom town house for $40,000.

PART III
Estate Agents, Developers and Time-Shares

Access Abroad
10 Manor Gardens
South Croydon
Surrey
CR2 7BU
01-686 1635

Alexanders Overseas Ltd
174 Edmund Street
Birmingham
West Midlands
B3 2HD
021-236 4422

Associated Spanish Properties
206 Upper Richmond Road
London
SW15 6TD
01-755 2150

Atkin International
The Stables
Hall Lane
Welbourne
Lincolnshire
LN5 0NN
(0400) 73139

Atlantic Leisure Group Limited
18 Hanover Street
London W1R 0EB
01-409 0571

Badet Sales Limited
14 High Street
Godalming
Surrey
GU7 1ED
(048 68) 28525

F H Barber and Company Limited
417-429 Northend Road
London SW6 1NX
01-381 0112

Barratts Multi-Ownership and Hotels Limited
Multi-Ownership House
6 Half Moon Street
London W1Y 7RA
01-629 2731

Beaches International Property Ltd
3/4 Hagley Mews
Hagley Hall
nr Stourbridge
Staffordshire
DY9 9LQ
(0562) 885181

Beach Villas Sales
55 Sidney Street
Cambridge
Cambridgeshire
CB2 3JN
(0223) 353222

Berdinat
163-169 Brompton Road
Knightsbridge
London SW3
01-589 4567

Bovis Abroad
Silver City House
62 Brompton Road
Knightsbridge
London SW3 1BW
01-225 0411

Bowlex
Westminster Bank Chambers
Market Hill
Sudbury
Suffolk
CO10 6EN
0787 313424

Bradley and Vaughan Overseas Ltd
34-36 The Broadway
Haywards Heath
West Sussex
RH16 3AL
(0444) 412551

Breading and Styles Limited
34 Watling Street
Canterbury
Kent
CT1 2UD
(0227) 454641

Breakaway Holiday Homes
14 West Street
Storrington
West Sussex
RH20 4EE
(09066) 2366

Brian A French and Associates Ltd
Suite 3
12 High Street
Knaresborough
North Yorkshire
HG5 0EQ
(0423) 867047

Broadway International Properties Limited
1st Floor
78 Bradford Street
Walsall
West Midlands
ES1 3QD
(0952) 620480

R M Brooker Limited
Yeoward House
P O Box 90
Trueman Street
Liverpool
Merseyside
L3 2BA
051-236 9306

Brulyn Sol Limited
74 Sackville Road
Hove
East Sussex
BN3 3HB
(0273) 720097

Burgau Holidays Limited
204-206 High Street
Bromley
Kent
BR1 1PW
01-460 8090

Canary Island Properties
Isabel House
46 Victoria Road
Surbiton
Surrey
KT6 4JL
01-390 7587

Casa Fina
Shamrock Quay
William Street
Southampton
Hampshire
SO1 7QL
(0703) 222363

Casitas Classiques Limited
Berkley House
121 Foxley Lane
Purley
Surrey
CR2 3HR
01-668 5555

Cassar and Cooper (Real Estate) Limited
P O Box 36
St Anne Court
Tigne Seafront
Sliema
MALTA
337096

Castle Villas Limited
4 Springfield Road
Kingston-upon-Thames
Surrey
KT12 2SA
01-549 5678

Catalan Property Services
Well House Yard
Hare Street
nr Buntingford
Hertfordshire
SG9 0EQ
(076389) 244

Chesham Group of Companies
9 London Road
Newbury
Berkshire
RG13 1JL
(0635) 49900

Chilcott White and Company
(Overseas)
125 South End
Croydon
Surrey
CR9 1AR
01-688 4151

Chrystal Brothers Stott and
Kerruish Ltd
Exchange House
Athol Street
Douglas
Isle of Man
(0624) 23788

Clovelly Country Club
Westminster Bank Chambers
Market Hill
Sudbury
Suffolk
CO10 6EN
(0787) 313424

Clowance plc
Clowance House
Praze an Beeble
Camborne
Cornwall
TR14 0PT
(0209) 831111

Cluttons
127 Mount Street
London W1
01-499 4155

Cowley Groves and Company Limited
43 Athol Street
Douglas
Isle of Man
(0624) 25888

Craigendarroch
Braemar Road
Ballater
Grampian
AB3 5XA
(0338) 55558

Crystal Properties Limited
The Studio
Hawley Manor
Hawley Road
Dartford
Kent
DA1 1PX
(0322) 93101

CISA Andorran Properties Limited
30 Notting Hill Gate
London W11 3HX
01-221 6843

Coope and Company (Properties) Limited
66/67 High Street
Lymington
Hampshire
SO41 9AI
(0590) 77971

Costa Blanca Villas
13/17 Newbury Street
Wantage
Oxfordshire
OX12 8BU
(02357) 65305

Cybarco Limited
Cybarco House
6 Dramas Street
P O Box 1653
Nicosia
CYPRUS
(02) 458058

David Ratel Limited
12 Vine Street
St Helier
Jersey
Channel Islands
(0534) 34521

David Scott International
Deerhurst House
Epping Road
Roydon
Harlow
Essex
CM19 5RD
(0279) 792162

De Vere Mews (London)
c/o Elliott Property Group
31 St George Street
London W1R 9FA
01-491 2677

East Midlands Overseas Owners Limited
774A Mansfield Road
Nottingham
Nottinghamshire
NG5 3FH
(0602) 200259

Effares Ltd
Sirdeane
Hogscross Lane
Chipstead
Surrey
CR3 3SJ
(0737) 553338
or
Aries Edifichi La Solana
Carretera d'Arinsal
La Massana
ANDORRA
(628) 36428/36432

Elliott Property and Leisure Group Limited
31 St George Street
London W1R 9FA
01-491 2677

Euroactividade SA
Apartado 24
P-8401 Lagoa Codex
Algarve
PORTUGAL
(82) 57262

Euro Property Advisers Limited
27 New Street
Salisbury
Wiltshire
SP1 2PH
(0722) 330847

Farrar Stead and Glyn
152 Fulham Road
London SW10 9PR
01-373 8425

Fincasol Limited
4 Bridge Street
Salisbury
Wiltshire
SP1 2LX
(0722) 26444
or
18 Queen Street
Mayfair
London W1X 7PJ
01-499 6187

Galerie International/
Juan Porsellanes SA
Business Design Centre
52 Upper Street
Islington Green
London N1 0QH
01-288 6062

George Knight Limited
P O Box 948
London NW3 5PY
01-435 2299

Giebels Propriedades Lda
Estrada Nacional 125
São Lourenco (8100 Almansil)
Algarve
PORTUGAL
(089) 95353

Gran Sol Properties
Summerville House
Heatley Street
Preston
Lancashire
PR1 2XB
(0772) 25587

Greenways International Limited
Greenways
Grubwood Lane
Cookham Dean
Maidenhead
Berkshire
SL6 9UB
(062 84) 2455

Griffiths and Griffiths LDA
c/o Griffiths and Griffiths
(Properties) Limited
130 High Street
Eton
Berkshire
SL4 6AR
(0753) 866012

Hamptons and Sons
6 Arlington Street
London SW1
01-493 8222

Hapimag, Comser International Ltd
Fairview Road
Timperley
Cheshire
WA15 7AR
061-904 9750

Headland Overseas Properties
67 Wellingborough Road
Rushden
Northamptonshire
NN10 9YG
(0933) 53333

Hilary Scott Overseas Limited
Church Lane
Barnham
West Sussex
PO22 0BP
(0243) 554319

Hispano Scott Property Limited
48 Queen Street
Exeter
Devon
(0392) 51699

Holmes and Leadbitter Spain SA,
Edif. Balmoral
11/22 Aved Ricardo Ricardo Soriano
Marbella
Malaga
SPAIN
(34) 52 775516

Homes in the Sun Limited
37 Headlands
Kettering
Northamptonshire
NN16 7ES
(0536) 84343

Horner-Hill French
16 East Street
Horsham
West Sussex
RH12 1HH
(0403) 210650

Imomarketing TCSA
P O Box 2751
Via Nassa 17
6901 Lugano
SWITZERLAND
(091) 57 3182

International Property Consultants
34 Ship Street
Brighton
East Sussex
BN1 1AD
(0273) 774098

Inter Spain Services (UK) Limited
Suite 2
66 High Street
Rayleigh
Essex
SS6 7EA
(0268) 775165

Italian Properties
The Old Telephone Exchange
Eckington
Pershore
Hereford and Worcester
WR10 3AR
(0386) 750133

Javea Homes Abroad Limited
17 Kirkdale Road
Harpenden
Hertfordshire
AL5 2PT
(05827) 61691

Jell Properties
152 Grand Drive
West Wimbledon
London SW20 9LZ
01-543 1922

JLM Estates
109 Kenilworth Road
Fleet
Hampshire
GU13 9AY
(0252) 621143

Jos Antonio Puche
4 San Fernando
03002 Alicante
SPAIN
34-6-5218038

La Rosa Properties
6 Rice Parade
Fairway
Petts Wood
Orpington
Kent
BR5 1EQ
(0689) 27300

Kingswear Park
Kingswear
Dartmouth
Devon
TQ6 0DA
(080 43) 5295

Leonard D Morgan Overseas
Chartist Tower Buildings
8 Dock Street
Newport
Gwent
NP6 1DX
(0633) 2133351

Solomon Levy
2/16 Kings Yard Lane
GIBRALTAR
(010) 350-77789

London Spanish Developments plc
153A Park Road
St John's Wood
London
NW8 7HT
01-586 9226
or
Harmony House
217 Stainbeck Road
Leeds
West Yorkshire
LS7 2LR
(0532) 688711

Lovell and Partners Limited
11 Smith Street
St Peter Port
Guernsey
Channel Islands
(0481) 23636

Mackinnon Hathway
Main Street
Kyle of Lochalsh
Highland Region
IV40 8AB
(0599) 4567

Malta Property Consultants Limited
6 Rashleigh Court
Church Crookham
Aldershot
Hampshire
GU13 0UQ
(0252) 617404

Marisol Villas
The Stables
Sugworth Lane
Radley
Oxfordshire
OX14 2HX
(0865) 739422

Martel, Maides and Le Pelley
The Property Centre
50 High Street
St Peter Port
Guernsey
(0481) 21203

McCabe and Lombard
5 Percy Place
Dublin 4
IRELAND
(01) 680466

Mediterranean Time Ownership Limited
Sovereign House
Lion Green Road
Coulsdon
Surrey
CR3 2NL
01-660 9275

Medway Properties (Overseas)
78 Wellingborough Road
Northampton
Northamptonshire
NN1 4DP
(0604) 39024

Meller Braggins and Company
3 Grove Street
Wilmslow
Cheshire
SK9 1EG
(0625) 527181

Mills and Company
Ryall Mead
Holly Green
Upton-upon-Severn
Hereford and Worcester
WR8 0PG
(06846) 3921

Henry Moog
P O Box 550509
Atlanta
Georgia 30305
USA
(404) 351-2200

Morecover Investments Limited
4/6 Whycliffe Road
Purley
Surrey
01-668 7771

MVE Developments Limited
27 High Street
Walthamstow
London
E17 7AD
01-520 3437

Nathaniels and Dicker Malta
38 Bodley Road
New Malden
Surrey
KT3 5QE
01-949 4134

Nova Leisure
27 Promenade
Southport
Merseyside
PR8 1QU
(0704) 32807

Overseas Residential Properties Ltd
Overseas House
5 Broadway Court
Chesham
Buckinghamshire
HP5 1DB
(0494) 791779

P and S Mills Limited
Castle Mews
29A Castle Street
Salisbury
Wiltshire
SP1 ITT
(0722) 334551

Perrymead Properties (Overseas)
55 Perrymead Street
London
SW6 3SN
01-736 5331

Peterson International Real Estates
33A Corn Street
Witney
Oxfordshire
OX8 7DG
(0993) 71187

Phillip Norris (International) Ltd
31 Market Place
Henley-on-Thames
Oxfordshire
RG9 2AA
(0491) 576889

Prestige Homes Limited
7 Euston Place
Leamington Spa
Warwickshire
CV32 4LL
UK926) 832220

Propertunities
Douglas House
Felnor Walk
Felixstowe
Suffolk
IP11 7DN
(0394) 272651

Prudential International Property Ltd
116 Kensington High Street
London W8
01-937 7244

Rainbow International Limited
Kingston House
7 London Road
Old Stratford
Buckinghamshire
M19 6AE
(0908) 567707

Ravenstone Securities Limited
James Sellars House
144 West George Street
Glasgow
Strathclyde
G2 2HG
041-332 3695

Reysea Properties and Leisure Ltd
14A Chine Avenue
Bitterne
Southampton
Hampshire
SO2 7JF
(0703) 443730

Robin Knight Overseas Limited
5 Market Place
Harleston
Suffolk
IP20 9AD
(0379) 853158

Sadler and Moreira LDA
Rua Direita 101
Praia da Luz
8600 Lagos
Algarve
PORTUGAL
(082) 69267

Samuel Harding and Sons Limited
Bath Lane
Leicester
Leicestershire
LE3 5BA
(0533) 22000

Smiths Gore International
Fielden House
Little College Street
London
SW1P 3SH
01-222 4054

Michael Spencer
93 Lonsdale Road
Oxford
Oxfordshire
OX2 7ET
(0865) 513926

Spratley and Company
33/34 Craven Street
London
WC2N 5NP
01-930 9803

Sturgis International
140 Park Lane
London
W1Y 4DN
01-493 1693

Sunwest Properties Abroad Limited
25 St Mary's Street
Thornbury
Bristol
Avon
BS12 2AA
(0454) 418888

Swoffer Shields and Partners Limited
Estate House
Ann's Place
St Peter Port
Guernsey
Channel Islands
(0481) 26131

Tavnerstar
Dominic House
171/177 London Road
Kingston-upon-Thames
Surrey
KT2 6RA
01-549 4251

Taylor Woodrow Homes Limited
c/o Hadfield House
Adrienne Avenue
Southall
Middlesex
UB1 2QZ
01-578 5757

The Melfort Club
Kilmelford
by Oban
Argyll
Strathclyde
PA34 4XD
(08522) 257

The Portuguese Property Bureau Limited
Algarve House
The Colonnade
Maidenhead
Berkshire
SL6 1QL
(0628) 32788

Theomaria Estates Limited
Valtetsiou 2-Limassol
P O Box 4282
Limassol
CYPRUS
(051) 72917

Timeshare Bourse Limited
Westminster Bank Chambers
Market Hill
Sudbury
Suffolk
CO10 6EN
(0787) 313424

Timesharing Ireland Limited
Fitzpatrick Castle Hotel
Killiney
Co Dublin
IRELAND
(001) 851533

Tourism Advisory Group
Westminster Bank Chambers
Market Hill
Sudbury
Suffolk
CO10 6EN
(0787) 313424

Tourist Office Cap D'Agde
Office Municipal du Tourisme et des Loisirs
Agde
BP 544
34305 Agde Cedex
FRANCE
(010) 33 67263858

Trafalgar House Residential
(Europe) Limited
1 Portland Square
Bristol
Avon
BR2 8RR (0272) 425001

Urbanizadora del Mediterraneo SAE
Valero Rivera 8
Almeria
SPAIN 04004
(951) 241077

Vernon Smith European
38 Bell Street
Reigate
Surrey
RH2 7BA
(0737) 246868

Villamed Properties (Cyprus)
5 Sleaford Road
Branston
Lincoln
Lincolnshire
LN4 1LL
(0522) 793065

Villa Owners Club Limited
19/21 High Street
Newmarket
Suffolk
CB8 8LX
(0638) 660066

Villas Abroad (Properties) Limited
55 York Street
Twickenham
Middlesex
TW1 3LL
01-891 5444

Villotel Limited
28 Grafton Terrace
London
NW5 4JJ
01-485 2733

Whiteway Properties
Suite 2
12 High Street
Knaresborough
North Yorkshire
HG5 0EQ
(0423) 865892

Wimpey Homes
241 Kings Road
London
SW3
01-351 3135

Wimpey Time Ownership
1a Springfield Road
Horsham
West Sussex
RH12 1HE
(0403) 56191

Woodside Europa Limited
Ingham
Bury St Edmunds
Suffolk
IP31 1NR
(0284) 84743

Useful addresses

Association of British Overseas
Property Agents and Consultants (ABOPA)
16 Jacobs Well Mews
London
W1H 6BD

British Association of Removers
(also International Federation of Removers)
277 Grays Inn Road
London
WC1X 8SY
01-837 3088

Federation of Overseas Property Developers,
Agents and Consultants (FOPDAC)
Imperial House
15-19 Kingsway
London
WC2B 6UU
01-240 5359
or
(0273) 690919

Foreign and Commonwealth Office,
Downing Street,
London
SW1A 2AL
01–233 3000

Law Society,
113 Chancery Lane,
London
WC2A 1PL
01-242 1222

National Association of Estate Agents
21 Jury Street,
Warwick
(0926)-496800

Royal Institution of Chartered
Surveyors,
12 Great George Street,
London
SW1
01-222 7000

Timeshare Developers Association,
23 Buckingham Gate,
London
SW1E 6LB
01-821 8845